Tortoise Wins the Race

The Race

THE SAFE AND SUCCESSFUL
ROAD TO RICHES

Brent Bullis

McLeod
P·U·B·L·I·S·H·I·N·G

Published in 1999 by McLeod Publishing Co. Limited
34 Lesmill Road, Toronto, Canada M3B 2T6

Distributed by:
General Distribution Services Ltd.
325 Humber College Blvd., Toronto, Canada M9W 7C3
Tel. (416) 213-1919   Fax (416) 213-1917
Email customer.service@ccmailgw.genpub.com

03   02   01   00   99   1   2   3   4   5

Canadian Cataloguing in Publication Data

Bullis, Brent
Tortoise wins the race: the safe and successful road to riches

ISBN 0-919292-06-2

1. Finance, Personal. 2. Investments. I. Title.

HG179.B84 1999   332'.024'01   C99-930093-8

Cover design: Angel Guerra
Text design: Tannice Goddard

THE CANADA COUNCIL | LE CONSEIL DES ARTS
FOR THE ARTS | DU CANADA
SINCE 1957 | DEPUIS 1957

*We acknowledge for their financial support of our publishing
program the Canada Council, the Ontario Arts Council, and
the Government of Canada through the Book Publishing
Industry Development Program (BPIDP).*

Printed and bound in Canada

Contents

List of Charts and Diagrams

Introduction

A s the Good Book says, "Of making many books there is no end." And who can argue with The Truth? There are certainly many types of financial planning books. Some, like the wildly best-selling *The Wealthy Barber*, are incredibly basic, almost an ABC of investing. Others seem far more complex and are, to a financial novice, what Rachmaninoff's Piano Concerto No. 3 — the one that drove the poor young pianist in the movie *Shine* into insanity — is to a child poking away at the black and white keys for the first time.

The purpose of this book is not to tell you what to do, but to open your mind to various possibilities, and to introduce you to new and promising ways of achieving financial success. Even if these methods are not always relevant to your personal situation, there's something to be said for awareness. After all, if you are unaware of them, how can you ever know if you should be using them? Although I have worked on financial planning with many thousands of people, almost none of them had heard of all the things we will discuss in this book before they met me.

I intend to provide you with a financial education. When you get a phone call from someone who says, "I have this fabulous concept for making money," after hearing the idea, I want you to be able to reply, "It's an interesting idea, and it's right/but it's not right for my situation, because of X, Y, and Z."

I have been an investment advisor in the province of Alberta for more than a dozen years. During that time, I was a branch manager for ten years and a provincial manager for four. I have worked very hard to help men and women of all ages to feel more secure, to grow in wealth, and to work towards fulfilling their dreams. (Which need not be merely financial, of course. To quote a joke, "Money cannot buy happiness; it can only buy you some of the things that can make you happy.")

I shall start with some basic concerns, such as how to choose a financial advisor, but I will also look at Systematic Withdrawal Plans, Family Tax Strategy plans, wise ways to guarantee your children's financial future, and much more.

I have made thousands of men and women a lot of money — and it wasn't through risking their money or my reputation. It was through careful, thoughtful, creative planning. That's why I've called this book *Tortoise Wins the Race*, with the explanatory subtitle, *The Safe and Successful Road to Riches*. If you wish to get rich very quickly, you'll have to play the lottery or visit a casino, and you'll need a very different book from this one.

This book is not about "playing the market" — a rather uncomfortable echo of "playing the lottery," I feel; it's about how to use knowledge and intelligence to help you fulfill your financial dreams — and still be able to sleep at night.

Chapter One

Why You Need a Financial Planner (and a Plan)

One thing that amazes me when potential clients first come in to see me is that they always have questions.

"Of course," you think. "Who *wouldn't* have questions for a possible new advisor?"

But it's the kind of questions they ask that are distressing:

- "I hear there's a promising new high-tech company going public soon; whaddayathink?"
- "So it looks like a bear market now, doesn't it?"
- "These stocks jump around too much, don't they? Are mutual funds my best bet?"

There is nothing specifically wrong with any of these queries. But they are all virtually dictionary definitions of "putting the cart before the horse." Even worse, none of these questions have much to do with The Process!

What do I mean by The Process? To answer that, let me tell you the kinds of questions I feel *should* be asked when a person first sits down with a possible financial advisor:

- How much money do I need when I reach the age of 65 in order to continue to enjoy my current lifestyle?

- What rate of return (that is, what annual percentage of growth in the value of my investments) do I need on my investments, in order to facilitate the retirement I someday hope to have?
- What type of risk goes with that rate of return?
- Will I be comfortable with that risk? (If you can answer yes to this question, that's fine. But if the answer is "no," you may not be able to afford the lifestyle you have envisioned. Or you might have to keep that job a few years longer.)
- Will my current investment plan get me where I need to be with a fair degree of certainty?
- What changes would you suggest I make, and why?
- How will these changes affect my current lifestyle and risk comfort levels?
- What do I have to do to be able to retire at the age of 60?

In other words, the first essential points all of you must consider — long before the terms *stocks, bonds, mutual funds, Canada Savings Bonds, Guaranteed Income Certificates*, or any others are mentioned — indeed, even before you visit a financial planner, are these:

- What do I want to achieve in my financial future?
- What is the risk associated with my being able to achieve those financial goals?
- What tradeoffs am I willing to make between my current lifestyle and my retirement aspirations?

AN INVESTMENT IS A
TOOL: NOTHING MORE OR LESS

One of the things many people forget is that any investment is merely a tool. It is a means to achieve an end. It is not an end in itself, merely the means to *get* there. (Yes, a castle on a Caribbean island might be a nice dream to strive for; but let's not get too far ahead of ourselves.)

Here's a pleasant little parable for you: You have hopped on a ship and sailed away on a journey. You don't have a rudder, unfortunately, so you will not be able to direct yourself towards or away from anything. You don't have a map, alas, so you don't know where you might be going — or how, or even if, you will ever manage to get there.

Bon voyage.

The problem is pretty clear: You failed to chart your course. You didn't know your destination or how to get there. It is not terribly surprising that boat designers created rudders and steering wheels, and cartographers created maps. What *is* truly surprising is how many millions — no, hundreds of millions — of men and women around the world hop on those rudderless, map-free boats nearly every day of their lives. Planners are always talking about "risks of the marketplace" and "acceptable risks for investments" with their clients. Yet here are all these people, leaping onto un-ruddered, map-challenged boats, ignoring the enormous risks of *not* charting a financial course in the first place! The *real* risk, in the world of finances — not even knowing your goals — far outweighs a teetering stock, a poorly managed mutual fund, or even an unstable market.

So, before you ask about a particular investment, or even visit a financial planner, you should come up with a basic framework (in other words, chart your course), and place investment strategies and individual investments into the framework that will help you get where you want to be, within the parameters you have set out. As I said — understand The Process.

Looking at the Big Picture

Whether you were taught to drive by a professional instructor or by your mom or dad, you were probably told to "look at the big picture." It was sound advice: Driving a car is more than turning the wheel left or right, or placing your foot on the brake. Is there a car just ahead of you? behind you? How close is it? Are you approaching a stop light? How far away is it? Is it turning red or already red? turning green or about to change? Is there someone about to cut into your lane from the left or the right? Is that a child on a bike rolling down his driveway, just ahead? Is the road slippery or dry?

A financial plan is all about looking at the big picture, not merely talking about initial investments. And that big picture involves those questions I listed for you earlier in this chapter. Because only when you have the big picture — your financial goals, the risks you are willing to take, etc. — can you work down into the "micros."

It is simply amazing how people will sit down with me in my office for ten minutes — *ten minutes!* — and expect me to tell them exactly how to set up their financial future. I have had a younger brother for more than three dozen years now, and he still does unexpected things. If I don't fully know my own brother after so many years, how am I expected to know someone fully after talking to them for only a half-hour, or even a full hour, on several occasions?

What I have learned is this: Quite often, people who are not sure what they want to do with their money, or how to think about their financial future, are perfectly willing to give up that responsibility to someone else! This fact is really quite astonishing, when you think about it. Grown men and women, who would *never* let another person tell them how to discipline their children, much less plan their dinner menu, are willing to (sometimes literally) push their life savings across the table to an almost perfect stranger and say, if not in so many words, "Here, you take care of this!"

But that is the worst possible thing you could do. You must empower yourself by gaining knowledge about investments, tax deferrals, market conditions, and more. Understandably, the world of finance is scary for many people. (How many of you, after all, wish to know how those trillions of ones and zeroes inside our computer allow you to e-mail your loved ones, or how the engine of your automobile makes the wheels rotate?) Yet it's one thing to find investment a bit daunting, and quite another to hand over responsibility for your life and future to someone else.

My clients are not voicing their discomfort, as they sit in my office, but their actions scream it loud and clear: "Here, you handle it, Bullis! You do everything!"

An essential reality, however, cannot be ignored: Nobody is going to take more time and effort with your financial dealings — and be more dedicated to making sure that you do well — than yourself. You've worked hard to earn that money, and no one knows how much it means to you, and what you want to do with it, better than you do. So, take the time to consider your financial future and your future needs and dreams before you even phone up an advisor or planner.

Your House Is Not Mine

Time for another parable: You are in your house one night when suddenly all the lights go out. It is pitch black, and you are in your bedroom, preparing to call it a night. You recall that there are flashlights in the kitchen, and you want to find them, so the children won't be too frightened.

Would you find this exceptionally dangerous? If your kids have continued to leave their in-line skates all over the place — not to mention their skateboards — then you might hesitate. But generally speaking, you shouldn't be too fearful to make your way down the stairs and into the kitchen.

Okay, now let's beam you up, *Star Trek*–style, out of your own bedroom and into my home, in beautiful suburban Edmonton, Alberta. It's still pitch black — I've had a power failure too — you're in a strange bedroom now, and you've got to find your way down to an unknown kitchen through hallways with which you are unfamiliar.

The latter case can be described as "risky." After all, you

don't know the layout of the bedroom, where the hallway is, the number of stairs down to the first floor, which way the kitchen is — or even if the Bullis family keeps flashlights there, or somewhere else.

Now, how can it be that finding flashlights in my home is quite risky for you, but doing the exact same thing in your own home is not risky?

It's simply a question of familiarity, is it not?

Moral of the story: Anyone who wishes to choose an advisor, or set up a financial plan, has to find somebody who is willing to devote the time and energy to empower *them* to obtain all the information they need to make correct decisions and choices!

Ninety-nine out of a Hundred Will Do Fine — If . . .

I have a belief that may surprise you: If one hundred people have all the information they need to make a decision, ninety-nine of them will make the correct one — 99% of the time. Yes, I really do believe this.

But as the American author Joseph Heller wrote, "There was only one catch, and that was Catch-22." In this case, the catch is that most of those hundred people (a) bring their emotions to bear on their decisions, and/or (b) do not have at their disposal all the information they need. And that two-part catch is a gigantic, even dangerous one.

What I have come up with is *not* a get-rich-quick scenario — not by a long shot. Successful financial planning takes time, and it takes patience. But if you ask the right questions (not the ones that new clients are forever asking me), you will find your experience incredibly satisfying, and you will end up with a more secure retirement than you ever imagined.

If you already have a portfolio of stocks, bonds, mutual funds, and so on, you and your prospective advisor should be able to look at that portfolio and have a serious discussion. Unfortunately, here is the kind of dialogue that often takes place:

BRENT: Why do you have this particular investment? When did you purchase it? What purpose does it fill in your financial plan, and is it still justified?

CLIENT: Well, my broker once phoned me and told me that I had some cash in my account, and that I should buy a few shares of General Consolidated Incorporated. Then its price dropped like a stone, so I've held it for the past six years, and I'm still waiting for it to go up!

BRENT (fighting back the smiles): So, what would have to happen for this investment to finally be sold?

CLIENT (not getting it yet): What are you getting at?

BRENT: You see, investments like this one are precisely the reason portfolios should be reviewed every three months. That way, you can make sure that your investments are still performing as expected; that your needs are still the same; and that each of your stocks and mutual funds are meeting the expectations that have been set out for them.

CLIENT: Cool!

BRENT: And if all of your investments are doing that, you should certainly keep them. But if they are not, you should look at moving them.

CLIENT (terrified): You mean . . . but . . . you can't mean that I should actually go ahead and . . .

BRENT: Calm down, calm down! Let me ask you a simple question. Why did you purchase all those shares of General Consolidated Incorporated?

CLIENT (with a "this guy must be nuts" look): Why, to make money, of course!

BRENT: Fair enough. So . . . did it?

CLIENT: Uh, er, well . . . no, it sure as hell did not!

BRENT: Okay, so it didn't. Lots of people lose money on at least some of their investments. So, what are you going to do about it now?

CLIENT (as if I have just asked him or her to sell a first-born child): What on earth can you mean?

BRENT: Let me rephrase. Why are you still sitting on this thing, after six years?

CLIENT: Well, I already told you — I lost money!

BRENT (a bit heartless, but that's my job at times): You are like so many other people! You have become emotionally attached to your investment, and it's rather touching. But it's not very financially clever.

There's an old saying: "You can't lose money until you sell." And like most old sayings, there is a smidgen of truth in it — but there's a lot of financial foolishness as well. Imagine going to a race track. You are thrilled to discover that there is a horse with the same name as the first friend you ever made, back in kindergarten. So you bet on it. It loses. You bet on it again. It loses again. You bet on it again. And every single time, it loses — not by a nose or a half-length, but by more and more lengths.

Do you continue to bet on the horse, throwing good money after bad?

The above dialogue and example demonstrate why, before you buy something, you should know what to expect from it. And if it fails to meet those expectations, you should know what you are going to do with it. That way, the problem does not linger on, like a bad cough (or a poor stock or a lame horse).

THE ADVANTAGE OF A BROKER, WHO IS *NOT* EMOTIONALLY TIED

A classic example of difficult decision-making for many people occurs when they have a stock recommended to them — let's call it Unlimited Potential. They heard from their friends that "it's sure to go up" — and it does! From $10.00 to $25.00! Then, alas, it tumbles to $7.50. Despite the drop, they still hold on to the stock, as if it were a sick child. And they come to me, and sheepishly ask, "What do I do with this thing?"

Well, 90% of the time, I don't have an answer for them. Why? Because they must get to the root of the problem:

Do you, as an investor, want to be faced with the endless decisions of when to buy and when to sell all these various investments? Investments that, in most cases, you know — and even care — very little about?

This is a profound dilemma. You see, when a person chooses to purchase individual stocks, he or she has usually (if unconsciously) decided to be a "stock picker and stock market timer." They have come to the belief that they will, with the occasional help of their broker or the assistance of various financial newsletters they receive, be able to leap in and out of the market skilfully and cold-bloodedly.

But stock market timing is difficult enough for the so-called experts — who are wrong up to half the time, often more — much less for the average person, and the decision to buy (and especially to sell) any stock is fraught with great emotion. Chances are, as soon as emotion enters any decision, people will make the wrong choice. That is why you must treat your money and your investments as if they are not yours. (Recall how often it takes a marriage counselor or psychotherapist to help people with their problems; most human beings have great difficulty coming to grips with their emotional baggage by themselves — or helping their closest loved ones with distress.)

Remember: A broker doesn't care. That's not totally fair; of course, brokers care — a little bit — but they don't care as deeply about your stocks and mutual funds as you do, any more than they care about your spouse, children, and pets as much as you do. And they certainly don't worry as much about whether you make or lose money on an investment, because they make their commission either way. I'm not being cynical here, simply realistic.

Are you comfortable with buying and selling your own investment vehicles? Are you impassioned or cool about your money and your investments? Do you love looking in the paper and checking the business pages? Do you love reading newspapers such as *The Northern Miner* and various other specific publications to help you make those snap decisions?

Or — as is far more likely — will you depend upon someone else to help make those decisions about when to buy, what to buy, when to sell, and so on?

If you are depending largely on somebody else, I have a few questions for you.

- How comfortable do you feel with the way you are currently handling your finances?
- Do you look into the future with confidence?
- Do you feel empowered, or are you dependent on the kindness of others?

Today is the first day of the rest of your life. If you are not comfortable, change what you are doing! Get a plan of action set up and follow it.

FORGET EVERYTHING YOU'VE DONE IN THE PAST AND START OVER

Forget everything you've been doing with brokers (and friends with "hot tips"), sit back, and start afresh. Ask yourself those crucial questions: "What do I feel comfortable with?" and "What's not comfortable for me?" The relationship with a financial planner is not unlike a marriage; you must ask, at the onset, "Do I trust this person?"

I would not give a single penny — even a worthless Canadian one — to someone I did not trust. So why would you give a broker thousands of dollars (even tens of thousands) along with the chance to profoundly affect your financial future, and those of your spouse, children, and grand-children? (I note the latter two to remind you of a fact that is too often ignored: A doctor may save your life; a clergyman may save your soul. But a financial planner or advisor — a good one — can greatly influence the lives of the next few generations of your family, in that you might be able to leave them enough money to go to costly universities, purchase homes and cottages, start businesses, donate generously to charities, and more.)

First comes trust. Then, you work through the next levels. It's absolutely essential that you analyze your portfolio by starting with the ground rules. And by that, I mean you must have a Financial Plan. Imagine hiring someone for a job, and then telling your new employee, "Just *do* it!"

"Do *what?*"

"Oh, there's *lots* of work to be done; just do it!"

"But I'm not sure exactly what you want me to . . ."

"Oh, yes — and if you don't do what I want you to do, I'm afraid I'm going to have to fire you!"

Pretty stupid, although this scenario certainly has TV sitcom potential. But I hope it makes my point very clear: No investment advisor or financial planner can operate under such vague guidelines; they must know specifically what the client wants and needs. And they can never know what you want and need, if you — the client — have not spent the time to truly decide such critical decisions.

That is what I mean by The Process. It is not like a light switch: Flick it, and the room brightens. It takes time, it's a journey, and it must be taken with someone you trust. (You hope that this journey might start through a referral from someone else who has taken the trip with the advisor or planner before you and has been pleased with the results.)

People rarely purchase a new automobile — which today costs an average of well over $20,000 — without doing some research, reading *Consumer Reports* and other quality magazines, talking to friends, and test-driving several different vehicles. In the same way, you should "test-drive" two or three financial advisors before deciding upon the one who could design your financial future (and potential financial security).

Alas, talk is cheap. There are thousands of very slick, very gifted salespeople, in the revered tradition of "that guy could sell ice to an Eskimo!" Fortunately or not, the selling of stocks and mutual funds is a business based on commissions; those who recommend these investment vehicles make their living from receiving tiny percentages of what they recommend — and what they sell — to you. It's capitalism in action, and there's nothing inherently wrong with that; few of us resent the sales clerk who urges us towards the purchase of a particular suit, tie, or even car, when we are well aware that they are probably on commission and make a few bucks with every sale.

But it's one thing to be steered towards Ralph Lauren or Mercedes-Benz and quite another to be pushed towards Stock A or Mutual Fund B; your future stability and your future dreams are at stake in your choice of investments — including the question of when you'll be able to retire (or possibly if you will be able to retire at all).

As a result, you must be very careful about whom you eventually choose as your financial planner; most in the business are pretty good, but there are those who are not (and who are still perfectly willing to accept the commissions on the equities and funds they recommend to you, in spite of their many failings). Naturally, you must safeguard yourself against choosing a flawed agent.

A catch comes up here with implications for your future: You must figure out The Process that you want and play it against The Process that your potential financial planner wants. Most brokers, salespeople, and planners spend their time interviewing you, then change their story to reflect what you appear to want. Eventually though, financial advisors will always gravitate towards their normal management style. This is understandable, but it can be bad for you. And if someone insists they can run thirty different strategies all at once — don't believe him or her for a second. They will inevitably come back to where they are, and how they act. Before you spend a lot of time talking about what you want, why not ask what they normally do, and what they usually recommend?

Ask what your prospective financial planner does for his or her clients. Only then should you decide if that's what you are looking for. Sure, everyone can change a little bit. But how much can they change — and will those changes be good for you and for your financial future?

Part of the purpose of this book is to give you things to look for, and questions to ask, always with a good sense and awareness of The Process involved. Everyone knows that if you have a good business plan — if you have a good process — you will probably end up being successful. (Unless your good business plan and good process entail selling buggy whips or electric typewriters.) Surveys show that if you purchase a franchise — whether it be a McDonald's, a Coffee Time, or a Ford dealership — your chances of success are something like 85%. After all, these various companies have track records; they make sure you have a quality product to sell, a good location and morale, financial and business support, and much more. But if you start your business from scratch, you could be one of the two out of three that fail within five years.

Here's the key: You must set up a financial plan, implement it, and update it with periodic reviews.

Chapter Two

Choosing the Right Planner

O nce you have laid out your preliminary Plan and have a sense of The Process, it is time to approach an investment advisor.

There are a number of categories of advisors and planners, and it's very important to know "where they are coming from." There are advisors with insurance backgrounds, who are essentially insurance agents. There are stockbrokers, whom I described in the previous chapter. And there are so-called independent financial planners, or mutual-fund salespeople.

Obviously, where your advisor "comes from" will invariably skew the kind of advice he or she will give you. When you take the kids to the movies, the rating system helps you assess whether the movie is appropriate: if it's a Disney cartoon, you have a decent chance of not having to cover their ears or eyes during the show; if it's rated R or X on the poster outside, you know you don't want to take the kids with you.

In the world of financial planning, it can be even easier and clearer. (After all, some of those films produced by Walt Disney can be pretty adult nowadays.)

- Insurance salespeople usually lean towards saving money inside insurance policies.

- Stockbrokers tend to recommend stocks, bonds, mutual funds, and other investment vehicles but generally "do" very little insurance.
- Mutual-funds salespeople predominantly handle mutual funds, although some will, of course, sell life insurance as well. And still others have the background and training to recommend stocks and bonds, too.

These general rules are starting to shift, and understandably so. (I'm old enough to remember when banks mainly handled chequing and savings accounts, mortgages, and business loans; today, you can buy insurance for your mortgage and the bank's own mutual-fund families — almost everything except a lube and oil for your car.)

More and more stockbrokers are starting to offer financial planning for their customers and are moving into the insurance industry; insurance salespeople are recognizing that there is more to life than whole life (or term) and are starting to sell some mutual funds. And then there are those segregated funds — which are tied up with insurance — that they are already selling.

As you can see, the guidelines are starting to blur, and the various categories of investment advisors are coming together. Nevertheless, each advisor still leans towards a particular attitude about how to invest, save, and plan. You must be aware of this bent and have a good sense of what you want when you look for an advisor.

We all have biases. Mine, as I discussed in the opening chapter, and as you can quickly gather from a glance at the back of this book, is towards The Financial Plan. I believe that everyone should have a financial plan to help them with their portfolio, their future, their retirement, and beyond.

I noted earlier that I see investment not as an end in itself, but as a means to an end — and that investments (be they stocks, bonds, mutual funds, GICs, CSBs, or whatever) are no more than tools. I often use a parable when I discuss this with my clients: You are alone in the woods, standing in front of your tent, about to make a fire. Suddenly a bear charges. You look down in a panic and see that you have two tools, both of great value: a shovel and a rifle. And the bear is getting closer. Which tool will you use?

It is pretty obvious in this case. The same situation is true with investments. How can you choose the proper investment, if you do not know the situation you are in?

If the situation is less clear, if a friend not far away in those woods calls to you, "I hear something! Grab anything!" and you reach for the shovel — and then a bear charges, you may well look back (from your bed in the hospital) and think regretfully, "Gee, I sure wish I had chosen the rifle.

This is an excellent analogy for the ultimate dilemma inherent in financial planning: If it takes five or ten years for you to recognize that you chose the wrong tool, how on earth will you be able to make changes? Although bears or robbers or serial killers may come into your life, they are extremely rare. But the need for financial planning — and choosing the proper tools or investments to guarantee a life of health, comfort, travel, and even prosperity — makes that choice of the "right tool" as essential and vital as what you reach for when a bear comes rushing towards you.

The problem is, after those five or ten years with the "wrong tool" (a bum stock, a poorly chosen insurance policy, a mutual fund that plummets and never recovers), you cannot go back and change things, because *you have lost time.*

And time is critical, as critical as the split-second choice between grabbing a shovel or a rifle, even though the time span here is in years and decades.

Let me explain. In the First Book of Corinthians, we read, "And now abideth faith, hope, charity, these three; but the greatest of these is charity." There is a similarly precious trinity of variables in investments: time, money, and rate of return. And the most important of these — like charity in Corinthians — is time. Why? Because time involves compounding. And compounding of interest is the miracle that can make investments grow, and grow, and grow, to stunning amounts, when given the time to do so.

It is essential that, if you wish to improve your financial situation, you make sure you are in the right place at the right time — and that you are using the correct vehicles for your plans and purposes. (And remember, rifles are *always* more satisfactory than shovels, when confronting charging bears.)

HOW TO FIND THE BEST TOOL(S) TO REACH FOR

The only way to make sure you are in the right place at the right time, and are choosing the right tools (investment vehicles), is to choose a financial advisor and have that advisor draw up a comprehensive plan for you.

I'll discuss this plan in detail in the next chapter. But choosing the investment advisor who will create the plan for you could be one of the most important decisions you'll make in your life.

The only way to figure out how much money you will need, how soon you will need it, and how much risk will be involved in achieving those numbers is to have a comprehensive plan created for you.

Naturally — and this is crucial — not all plans are the same, any more than all advisors are. I urge you to interview — yes, interview, as if you were considering them for a job you need to have filled — at least three or four advisors. After all, this is a vital decision. You are choosing someone you are going to trust, who will help you achieve what you want to achieve, who may well mould your future happiness and the happiness and monetary prospects of your descendants.

As I noted in Chapter One, if you are the type who loves to do a lot of the planning alone, merely dealing with a stockbroker (who will buy and sell for you) may be sufficient. But you'll never know for sure until you go through The Process.

I urge you to do the following before you choose an advisor: Talk to a life insurance agent. Talk to a mutual-fund salesperson or an independent financial planner. Talk to a stockbroker. Maybe even talk to more than one in each area. And interview them.

Go through The Process. Find out what system they use, what system you are comfortable with, which strategies you feel most at home with.

Only then, when you have learned all of these things, can you safely and wisely proceed to entrust someone with your money and with helping you plan your financial future.

There are professional designations the men and women working in each of these areas can earn. It's helpful if you understand what these designations entail and what steps each of these professionals have gone through to achieve their goals.

In the case of independent mutual-fund salespeople, look for a CFP, which stands for a Certified Financial Planner, and RFP, which stands for Registered Financial Planner.

A Certified Financial Planner must take six courses in order to gain those credentials. Once they've passed these courses, they must submit a financial plan to the Financial Planning Standards Council of Canada (FPSCC), which awards them the designation of CFP. When they have earned the CFP, they can write a six-hour examination to achieve an RFP designation.

The CFP is an internationally recognized designation, begun in the U.S., with chapters in many countries. The RFP is recognized in Canada as the top financial-planning designation on the independent side of the financial-planning field.

Life-insurance agents earn a degree called the CLU, or Chartered Life Underwriter. The CLU program was established for the life insurance professional with a "solid track record dealing in most fields of life and health insurance who wants to provide even more efficient and professional service." They study these areas: planning for the business owner and professional, group benefits, disability, applied estate planning, and advanced tax law.

After successfully earning the CLU designation, an agent may go on to enrol in the Chartered Financial Consultant course of study. The CHFC designation "demonstrates excellence in financial planning," because agents learn how to create a comprehensive financial plan that addresses "all of the client's life insurance, wealth accumulation, and estate planning objectives." They study such subjects as advanced tax law, advanced retirement planning, advanced capital accumulation, applied financial planning, and more.

For a stockbroker to be qualified as a Financial Planner, he or she must pass parts one and two of the PFP (Professional Financial Planning) course.

The CFA (or Chartered Financial Analyst) designation allows an analyst to be a portfolio manager — someone who can legally manage a pension fund or mutual fund. The Institute of Chartered Financial Analysts awards the CFA to financial analysts who can pass examinations that cover everything from economics to portfolio management. In addition to passing the three levels of the CFA examination, a financial analyst must have three years of experience and meet other requirements to qualify for CFA.

A good advisor does not have to be a financial planner — but in my view, a good advisor should follow the principles of financial planning. There are many advisors who have been around for a long time who have never found the time to take all the courses necessary for "the paper on the wall." They should, but they are still excellent at what they do.

On the other hand, there are a lot of men and women out there who do have their financial planning certificates, but whom I wouldn't trust with a penny of my money. As we all know so well from professionals who have crossed our paths in life, just because someone has the credentials does not mean that they are good at what they do.

Chapter Three

The All-Important Financial Plan

Not all financial planners are the same (big surprise there), and not all financial plans are the same (ditto). Which is why you must look carefully at what you want from The Plan. To be blunt, what is its purpose?

Naturally, what you will want to create in a financial plan will vary greatly, depending upon your age and your expectations. If you are just starting out with a new family, a financial plan is going to concentrate more on asset accumulation: If you save X amount of money, and average an annual return of Y, you should expect Z money at the age of retirement — whenever that may be.

Interestingly, financial plans become exceedingly important when you are around the age of 50. It is then that men and women start to realize that they are mortal. Before that age, many people — far too many, in fact — do not save as much as they should, and they become aware of this frightening fact rather late.

Still, there is no question that in their 40s and 50s, most people rather abruptly start looking to the future. And it is at this point (how much nicer if they had thought of this when they were in their teens or 20s — more on that soon), that they ask those vital questions I noted in the opening chapter, which are worth repeating endlessly throughout this book, and throughout your life:

- When can I retire?
- Can I retire when and where I want to?
- What rate of return do I need on my investments to be able to retire when I want to?
- How much money do I have to save in order to retire when I want to?

How you arrive at the answers is what I like to call the Completion Backwards Principle. But first . . .

THE KINDS OF PLANS YOU'D BE WISE TO AVOID, AND THOSE YOU SHOULD FOLLOW

Once you have recognized that you need a financial plan, you must question what this plan encompasses. Looking around, you will see many advertisements by men and women who claim they "provide financial plans."

That sounds just fine. But these plans often consist of a single-page report that proclaims, "If you save $25 every month for thirty-five years, you will end up with X number of dollars!" As you can imagine, I do *not* consider this worthy of the description "A Financial Plan."

There are others who can run two hundred pages on their computers, word processors, or electronic spreadsheets that leave you with the feeling that by the time you reach page ten, you will not remember what you read on page one. You take it home . . . it sure looks impressive . . . you file it . . . you never see it again. Nor do you hear from its creator again.

Which leads to the question, what is the purpose of a financial plan? Since this question, unlike so many of my others, is not rhetorical, let me give my own definition of this essential document, and then list what I believe a high-quality financial plan should involve.

The purpose of a financial plan is to set out a financial strategy, or, at the very least, chart a direction that you wish to follow. It should:

- Be something you can refer to easily to make sure you are remaining on course;
- Be easy to understand;
- Set you up with a line of reasoning or thought that you can feel comfortable with over time;
- Be able to help you get where you want to be, when you want to be there.

In theory, at least, a financial plan should be a very simple document. This does not mean, of course, that it should lack numbers; indeed, it may contain quite a few. Some clients may find these numbers a bit complicated and difficult to comprehend. But they are simply a way of demonstrating that you can reach your financial goals, and that if the market or any personal emergency or change of status forces you to stray from those goals, your plan can return you to the right path. This path, necessarily, is always anchored in logic.

The first thing I do is request that a client fill out a form with all relevant information: Do you have investments? Where are they? Do you have a home? Is there a mortgage on that home? What is your marital status? Do you have any children and what are their ages? (See Appendix One for a sample of this form.) There are certain materials you will need to bring to the meeting with your financial advisor. They are:

- Photocopies of your most recent Pension Estimates or Records of Contributions and Service.
- Photocopies of all RRSP, other savings plan, and investment statements from *all* financial institutions.
- Photocopies of CCP contribution statements and benefit estimates.

- Photocopies of previous year's income tax Notice of Assessment indicating your allowable RRSP contribution for this year.
- The amount of the Cash Surrender Value of life insurance. This is the total *current* cash surrender value *including* accumulated policy dividends.

(The above information is required for both husband and wife in the case of a married couple.)

You should also consider the following points:

- The age at which you wish to retire.
- The annual *after tax* income you desire in retirement. Think about the amount of take-home pay you now have and adjust for changes in lifestyle between now and retirement, and after retirement.
- Do you intend to spend your savings and investments during retirement or leave an estate to your heirs and beneficiaries? How much would you leave to your heirs?
- How long should you plan for (i.e., how long should your savings last)? Normal life expectancies are 74 years for men and 81 years for women. We recommend that you plan for your savings to last at least until age 90.

The form that your advisor uses may vary somewhat; however, you should expect to relay all of the information you see in the appendix. Many planners use a questionnaire to determine risk tolerance as well. These forms, too, are varied, and I have not included one.

All this information is necessary, even though many people find it difficult to share (especially with someone with whom they may have spoken for only a few minutes) so much extremely personal information. If it makes a client more comfortable, most financial advisors will be happy to sign a paper that declares, "If you decide not to proceed with me as your financial advisor, all originals of this document will be given back to you, and all photocopies will be destroyed." A declaration of that kind in advance may relieve any awkwardness or discomfort on your part. See it as a kind of pre-nuptial agreement, if you wish; it seems to be working for Barbra Streisand and her recent husband, James Brolin!

All kidding aside, trust should not be taken lightly. If a financial planner or advisor is taking all that time to work with you in order to set up a financial plan, this plan should *never* be a sales tool. It is being set up, after all, to help give you direction, to empower you to achieve your desired future. And if you are not fully open with the advisor about where your investments are, and what you plan to do with them, or about any debts you may have incurred, the whole process becomes a mockery. It doesn't help you, and it is certainly a waste of time for everyone involved.

If you are going to enter a relationship based on trust and respect, you must be able to provide full disclosure of your financial and personal status. And if you do not feel comfortable doing this with a particular person, he or she is clearly not the person you should be dealing with as your prospective financial advisor. Move on and look for someone else.

Which brings me to my famous . . .

Completion Backwards Principle

Traditionally, families pay off all of their bills and save what they can, hoping they will have enough to retire on. When they reach 55, if they do not have enough money to retire, they work until they are 60; if they still do not have enough, they work until they can afford to retire.

The Completion Backwards Principle looks at retirement saving from another direction. This concept is not as complex as it may sound. It's really not that different from the traditional method of saving. In this method, you look at the age you want to retire and work backward to the present to see what you have to do to facilitate your retiring at a specific age with a specific income and lifestyle.

Let's look at an example, based these assumptions:

1. Current age: 50.
2. Inflation: 3% a year.
3. Yearly increases in employment income until retirement: 3%.
4. Rate of return on RRSP (all earnings re-invested): 8%.
5. Retirement income: based on 70% of current income, adjusted for inflation.
6. Current income: $70,000.
7. Retirement savings are to last for twenty-five years, from the ages of 65 to 90. Funds are to be used up by age 90.
8. RRSP investment made in full January 1 of each year.
9. Calculation excludes CPP/QPP and OAS benefits.
10. No company pension plan.

To have a retirement income equal to $49,000 a year in today's dollars, this fictitious man would need to have saved $1,144,820 in an RRSP by the age of 65.

This simple example starts at the end, with how much the man needs to save to retire. We list what we know, such as income and what percentage of it he thinks he'll need annually at retirement, then make some educated guesses about inflation and how long he is likely to need this income. Then we calculate the lump sum of money needed to give him that annual income.

He may have some money already saved in an RRSP, so we would need to project the growth of that investment at an assumed rate of return to age 65. This amount would then be subtracted from the $1,144,820 needed in all RRSPs. If there is a shortfall, he would have to calculate the monthly or annual savings needed to make up the shortfall.

Maximizing your RRSP may not get you to your goal, so you may have to save money outside your RRSP as well. There is, of course, a difference in tax treatment, which is why it's best to relate these numbers to an after-tax income.

Be conservative in your calculation of that rate of return! True, you may have been rejoicing in those rich 15% annual returns from your stocks and mutual funds in the mid-1990s, but rates probably won't be so high over the next decade or two. Unless you plan to keep working and earning until the age of 80, it's best to figure an 8% or 10% annual return on your investments. For that matter, if you are moving towards retirement and have a number of bonds and GICs in your portfolio, I'd urge you to guesstimate more in the range of a 4% to 7% return on such investments.

You can see what I am recommending here: Always guess lower than you might feel you can expect from your investments; it's better to be pleasantly surprised when you retire than to discover you may have to hold down that job or take on others for a few more years. I always assume that my clients will be making a lower rate of return than expected (by me or by them), and that there will be a higher rate of inflation than has been predicted by experts. Pad both sides, for safety's sake.

Depending on the types of investments you choose, these financial vehicles will, over time, perform in a certain manner. You don't expect a leopard to act like a zebra (or to change its spots into stripes, for that matter). For example, if you invest in equities, or stocks, it is fair to expect a 10%, 15%, even 20% drop in the value of your investments every three to five years. That's been the pattern over the past century, and there is little reason to believe it will change. (In spite of the shock for many at the time, the wild volatility and heavy corrections on the U.S. and Canadian stock exchanges in the summer and fall of 1998 were really no surprise to people who follow and understand the way the market has always worked throughout its history.)

Corrections happen. If you play hockey, you must expect

lots of body checks, if not the occasional tooth-loosening slam. If you buy stocks, you must expect corrections and be prepared for them. If you can't handle those corrections (or those dental visits), stay off the ice, and get out of the stock markets. To repeat a cliché, forewarned is forearmed.

It is not my intention in this simplistic example to describe a full-blown financial plan. There are hundreds of variables we did not discuss, such as indexing of pensions, company pension plans, CPP and OAS payments, tax treatment of non-RRSP investments, possible downsizing of homes, the effect of inheritances, and so on. Because of the impact of these variables, you really need a computer program to help design your plan. It will enable you to examine different outcomes when you change a variable and is much easier than trying to do it with a pen and paper.

You must know what you wish to achieve financially by the time you retire, what you must do in order to achieve that, and the risks associated with reaching that financial goal. Then you can set up your portfolio to achieve your goals. This is the easiest kind of accumulation financial plan — it shows you that you have to save X amount of dollars in order to retire on what you want, where you want, and when you want.

Uh-Oh. It Ain't Always So Easy

Retirement can be a wonderful thing. Of course (Catch-22, again), your investments at that point (and/or your pension, savings, etc.) have to keep working for you to allow you to enjoy your new lifestyle.

Unfortunately, at this point, the pitfalls can begin to grow wider. Say you are presently a senior citizen, and you have a few hundred thousand dollars invested in GICs that are earning 10%. You are living off $10,000 a year per each hundred thousand saved, and life has been good.

Now the GICs come due, and the interest rate being offered is 4%. Suddenly you've been hit with some real problems. If you're 70 years of age, there's not much you can do about it, is there? You can look at reverse mortgages, perhaps. But is your pension fully indexed upon retirement? CPP, for instance, is fully indexed against inflation.

If your pension is indexed to, say, 60% of the inflation rate, and there is a history of longevity in your family, you are going to have to make up for the shortfall in your pension as you move through your 70s and 80s (since it's not fully indexed over the years). Unless, of course, your financial planner has wisely plotted in and made allowance for the reduction in purchasing power of that pension over time, and has made sure that you, the client, are comfortable with that reduction.

Clearly at some point — and this varies with each person — your income requirement will fall. You may travel less, give up driving, move to smaller premises, not eat out as much, and so on. All these factors, and many more, should be considered in the plan.

As you can see, the topics I've been discussing are not really that complicated. It's just that there are various things you should be aware of — from (inevitable) inflation rates to (expected) stock market corrections, to the (unpredictable) fluctuations of interest rates and more. And I do not mention these many variables here to frighten or discourage you.

Remember how scary it was the first time you tried to ride a bike — with or without training wheels. You probably fell and bruised your knees, and your pride may have been bruised as well. After a few tries, however, you didn't even think twice about leaping on the bike. Investing, financial planning, and working "backwards" towards retirement are really the same; you just have to learn to deal with a different environment.

If your pension is not fully indexed to inflation, your other investments will simply have to perform a little better. Or you must have a little more money invested. Or you may have to choose financial vehicles that might carry more volatility, but could have more financial reward as well.

Achieving the lump sum required to get you to a satisfactory, dreamed-of retirement is only the first part of the battle. The second part is ensuring that you maintain that purchasing power over time — because you won't be able to go back to work, or more likely, you simply won't want to.

In my opinion, a good financial plan should have a year-by-year breakdown of exactly what your retirement will look like. True, anyone who has ever done a projection knows that the further ahead you project, the less meaning it has. For this reason, it is critical that the entire retirement plan is completely reviewed every two or three years, at the very least. And it really should be looked at every year to make sure that you are on track.

INSIDE THE **RRSP** OR OUTSIDE THE **RRSP?**

The above, essentially, is what a financial plan is all about. We've charted how to get there (sometimes backwards, I admit), based on what you have said you want or need at the time of retirement, assuming certain inflation and risk factors along the way. We have taken a look each year at your situation and have decided how much you should take out of your RRSP at retirement.

Sadly, many people find that when they reach retirement age their only savings is the money they managed to save in their RRSPs. As we know, RRSP withdrawals are fully taxable. Large withdrawals can become prohibitively expensive when taxes are taken into consideration.

You all know the reason: If we are at the top marginal tax bracket, our friends at Revenue Canada insist on taking approximately 50% of every dollar we make in income or take out of our RRSPs. This rate varies a bit by province, but it's certainly a lot more than the 38% (or so) top bracket in the populous and wealthy country to the south of us.

Most Canadians look to retirement as a time when all of their non-tax-deductible debts will be paid off — no more car payments, mortgage payments, etc. If all your savings are in your RRSPs, how will you purchase a car? Are you going to drive the same car for thirty more years? Can you justify taking $80,000 out of your RRSP to pay for a $40,000 car? (Remember, Revenue Canada would take half of the $80,000 in taxes.) If you don't want to do this, you are back to being forced to make all large purchases on a payment plan. This need not be a negative thing to do; however, make sure that your plan is adjusted to reflect the new reality.

If you do not want to be in the above situation, you must save some money outside an RRSP. This after-tax money will give you more flexibility in how you make your purchasing decisions. The RRSP is there to deal with necessities when you retire, but it is *not* meant to deal with the lump-sum pleasures that we all want during retirement.

That brings us back to the accumulation part of the financial plan. Let's say that the plan we set out demanded only that you maximize your RRSP payments each year. Now that you've had an opportunity to look into the future and see what retirement may look like, you realize you'll have the money you will *technically* need, but you will lack the flexibility you desire. So there is a further requirement to be fulfilled. You really will need some money saved outside your RRSP when you've retired.

How are you going to achieve this while you are still working? (Assuming that you still are.) Most working families have limited budgets to work with — so where is the extra money going to come from? Does this mean that you still maximize your RRSP payments?

What do you do?

If you listen carefully, the Plan is making suggestions to you. As you go through the years, and work with your plan, your path should become obvious to you. (Notice that I have not even mentioned what I want, as an investment advisor; I've made no money, as yet. All I've been doing is showing you things that might affect your life, and that you might wish to change.)

This brings us back to the choice of investments. There is no such thing as the perfect investment or investment vehicle. If there were, you would buy it in a flash at your local convenience store, and I would be out of a job.

You, Your Spouse, Your Children, and Your Future

Because it's your future I've been talking about here, everyone in your family should be fully involved in your financial planning and The Financial Plan. In most families I meet, there is one spouse who is more mathematically inclined than the other, and this imbalance can pose a risk. Life isn't fair, as you know, and if the husband or wife who is most interested in planning the future dies, the surviving spouse can be quite literally left out in the cold, not understanding why certain decisions have been made.

For this reason, I find it critical that both spouses are involved in creating The Plan. Indeed, if my clients are in their 70s, I recommend that one or two of their children are also involved, so that they know what is there, what to expect, and what their parents are doing to protect themselves and very possibly assist in their children's future.

Children — and the less mathematically inclined spouse — need not necessarily know all the figures involved, but they should have at least a bit of understanding, because there must be continuity. Do you aspire to leave money to your children and/or grandchildren? If so, this should be factored into The Plan. But what is the most efficient way to benefit their lives and avoid a nasty swipe by the tax man?

Should you be giving with a warm hand (in other words, when you are alive), or with a cold hand (guess)? Do you wish to make arrangements for these gifts in your will?

These are not the sorts of decisions you can make by sitting down for a few minutes, or even a half-hour, with a financial planner. A true financial plan takes time, and it takes effort. And if you are to spend that much time with a planner or advisor, you must ask him or her questions worthy of all that time and effort:

- What are we going to do with this plan, after I leave this office?
- Am I going to hear from you again? And if so, when?
- When do I get an updated plan?
- What is the schedule of events that will happen over time, and what should I expect?

Some advisors will say to their clients, "Oh, I'm buy-and-hold for the long run; that's my strategy; you needn't hear from me again. Your investments have been made; they are excellent ones; that's it; bye-bye!"

Are you really comfortable with that?

As you can guess, I am not. You have to make sure that your expectations match what is happening to your investments. Then, over time, if things change — and they will change — you will want to make sure that you review your plan on a regular, on-going basis, and, if necessary, upgrade the plan.

For example, if inflation numbers have not worked out as expected and predicted — and most readers will remember when inflation hit the high teens in Canada, and mortgage rates the low twenties — you have to redo the plan and change those inflation numbers to match your changed expectations. Or maybe you will have to adjust the rates of return.

Your Plan becomes a reflection of your dreams and the path to achieving them. This is why, when I look at someone's portfolio, I should be able to point to any investment and ask, "Why is that one there? What's the purpose of it? What is the risk?"

A plan is necessary to make sure that everything integrates; everything should relate to the ultimate Plan. Throughout this book, I hope to show you different strategies to make your plan — your financial future — more successful, less risky, more satisfactory. I want to show you different investments, as well, and different ways to accomplish what you want.

The caveat is, I haven't met any of you. So I'm going to discuss many different strategies, many different ideas. Some may be appropriate for your situation, and others may not.

IT'S ALL ABOUT POWER, REALLY

One of the more memorable lines of the 1992 presidential election in the United States was spoken when the advisors of Bill Clinton joked, "It's the economy, stupid!" They rode that attitude to victory over then-President Bush, who seemed not to be aware of this essential fact that was affecting all Americans far more than any war in the Gulf.

I have created a similar one-liner to explain how vital financial knowledge is to all of us: "It's empowerment, [so you won't be] stupid!" Creating a financial plan can empower you. It gives you power over yourself and over your destiny. It gives you control — which is essential, because there is nothing worse than that uneasy, nagging feeling that "I've done something wrong with my money!" or "I should have acted on such-and-such an investment, and I never did!" Life is simply too short to worry about the countless choices you could have made.

We all know there are no guarantees in life. You could lose your job. Illness could strike a member of your family. (I'm sounding like the traditional life insurance salesman here!) *Things happen*, to clean up a commonly used expression.

But when you have a financial plan, you at least have a

course; you know the direction you're going. I can't promise that it will be a straight line — from small, monthly investments to great wealth; from today to retirement and beyond — which is why I insist that every little while, you must review your plan, to bring it back on course.

Having a financial plan allows you to spend the majority of your time on the things that really matter: family, religion, health, relationships, maybe the occasional game of golf.

What's important in life is the journey you take. The title of a lovely book of reminiscences by Leonard Woolf, the husband of the great novelist Virginia Woolf notes, *The Journey Not the Arrival Matters*. And it's true. The destination is, of course, death, but a lot of good living and experiences can occur along the way.

The purpose of The Plan is to find that delicate balance between giving people what they want now without sacrificing the future, and giving them what they will want and need in the future without sacrificing (too much of) the present.

Look at your friends and acquaintances who appear to really "have it together." The happy, centred people of the world usually know where they are going, and the purpose of the journey they are on. A good financial plan can buy each of us that freedom, so we can enjoy our lives and continue to enjoy them beyond retirement age. And freedom is certainly a wonderful thing to achieve, with financial freedom being a necessary part of that achievement.

We should not have to worry about our financial situation. Money, as I love to remind my clients, is a means to an end, not an end in itself, and most of us take it far too seriously. Many of my clients chuckle when they hear me say this, and exclaim, "Come on, Bullis! It's rather strange that you, a money man, suggest that money is *not* the most important thing!" I remind them that, if I die tomorrow, my life won't be measured by my net worth, by how much money I've managed to stow away. People will look at my children, my marriage, my contribution to my church, and my work in various organizations. That is who Brent Bullis is (or was, should I really go tomorrow!).

Hence, we need The Plan: something that will show each of us where to find (and create) our happy equilibrium, so we can truly enjoy a full, satisfying, and worry-free existence.

CHAPTER FOUR

The Investment Cycle

A very attractive part of my job as a financial advisor, and one I really enjoy, is that I meet many interesting people. But very few of them really understand what drives the market, and what causes market cycles to occur.

Just pick up any daily newspaper in Canada, or anywhere else in the world for that matter, and here's what you see: We are reaching the tail end of the bull market cycle! Or, possibly the same week: Beginning of new bull market foreseen! Or, everyone's favourite: We are now in the middle of a bear market cycle. (When you think "bear," think claws, tearing of flesh, ripping of teeth, loss of financial happiness.)

Thanks, but no thanks.

What does all this mean in English, as opposed to financialese, these endless terms that financial advisors are always using? (And you wondered why medical doctors love to use Latin in their description of various diseases and conditions? It's to confuse us, thereby making us reliant upon them.)

I've devised a simple little illustration that explains how the investment cycle works. You will need to keep referring back to it as you read through this chapter. The circle in the diagram represents a clock. At twelve o'clock, interest rates are at their peak. Moving to the right, interest rates fall until six o'clock, the point when interest rates are at their lowest. Continuing to move clockwise, interest rates rise again, returning to their peak at twelve o'clock.

Diagrams are designed to be simple; unfortunately life is not as obliging. There is no set time frame for an investment cycle, and one cycle is never the same as another. Interest rates may rise or fall very quickly, or very slowly. They may stay low or high for a very long time. There is no magic number that indicates the current position of the investment cycle. As a result, economists and financial advisors relate the current environment to situations in the past in an attempt to explain what might happen in the future. Because this is anything but an exact science, the public is constantly bombarded with conflicting theories and suggested courses of action.

It's important to me that you understand how and why the investment cycle works, so you can build a foundation for a thoughtful financial plan. I explain various strategies throughout this book that depend upon you having a solid understanding of why events are happening and what their potential implications are. Throughout this chapter I will relate various points on the investment cycle to experiences in the past. We will look at who has benefitted and who has not. I will also show you where you should be invested, based on the general market conditions around you.

My goal is not to turn you into an economist, but to help you develop a keen sense about the investment cycle that will prevent you from making unwise investment decisions.

THE CYCLE BEGINS AT TWELVE O'CLOCK

Here's how the investment cycle works. Let's start with the early 1980s, when interest rates were high. (Find the top of the clock in the diagram on the next page; we're going to move to the right as we go.) Who was happy in those years? Seniors, of course! They just *loved* it. They had 100% guaranteed GICs — guaranteed investments — yielding them 10%, 12%, 14%,

THE INVESTMENT CYCLE

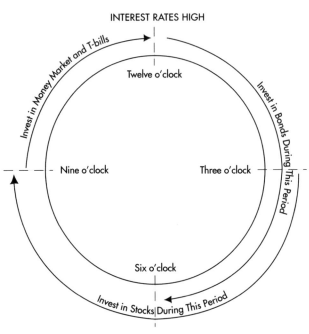

INTEREST RATES HIGH

Twelve o'clock

Invest in Money Market and T-bills

Invest in Bonds During This Period

Nine o'clock

Three o'clock

Six o'clock

Invest in Stocks During This Period

INTEREST RATES LOW

and even higher. They had no risk, and they were laughing their way to and from the bank. That's why so many Canadians eagerly purchased and held GICs and term deposits during those high-interest, high-inflation years. Even Canada Savings Bonds (CSBs) were paying double digits, as were many other bonds. These investors were as happy as prospectors sitting in the middle of a broad vein of gold.

We know who was happy back then. Who was unhappy?

What if you had a mortgage on your house back then? Suddenly, mortgage rates shot up as high as 23%. If you found it necessary to renew your mortgage, you must have struggled with how to continue making mortgage payments. It was incredibly difficult to sustain mortgages in those years, and the average working Canadian was hammered by those terrifying interest rates.

When interest rates reached such heights, how many average Canadians were about to go out and purchase new cars? Or dishwashers? Or dining room sets? Or fashionable new winter coats?

Most Canadians now believe in the buy-now-pay-later world. Unlike previous generations, who believed in having cash in hand before they would buy anything, we look for Instant Gratification. We freely hand over plastic to pay for something, whether or not we can afford to pay the bill in the near future.

In the early 1980s, borrowing costs and the costs of financing went through the roof. Consumers who were faced with this market either cut back on purchases or bought goods and then found that they could not afford to continue paying the servicing costs for them. And the companies who were manufacturing those cars, those dishwashers, those dining room sets, those new winter coats? When demand dropped, many workers lost their jobs.

What you saw at the height of high interest rates was a lot of ugly things: Unemployment increased dramatically. Companies either went bankrupt or downsized savagely. And if your friends lost their jobs, how confident did that make you with regard to your *own* employment? Did you rush out and purchase a new house at those high mortgage rates, and extend those gigantic payments over a long period of time?

Hardly. You pulled in the reins and spent less: "Listen, honey, we have to cover these Visa and MasterCard payments as soon as we can; we've got to avoid these giant interest rate payments. We've got to tighten our belts. And I'm not so sure about my employer, and whether I can hold onto my job much longer. Things are slowing down, orders are way down, and I just might be terminated."

It's easy to figure out that people who are terminated are not going to be buying a lot of new "toys."

You can see that a business cycle can often become a vicious circle: People stop spending, and companies produce fewer goods because there is less demand. And the high supply and piled-up inventories drive prices down.

What happens during this painful period? Most business owners keep producing, in the hope that the trend will start to reverse. (Contrary to popular belief, most business people are family people, just like you and me.) So inventory levels usually start to increase.

In periods of dramatic recession such as I have described above, when the economy is essentially stalled, you hear on TV and read in the newspapers about inventory levels, the unemployment rate, and interest rates.

It really is a vicious circle to get out of. And I didn't even mention that the price of stocks has dropped, because profits are down for all those corporations who have gone public and are listed on the world's exchanges; they haven't been selling their goods, so they are making a lot less money.

Now, if *you're* in need of money, what's the first thing you are going to "cash out"? Something that is marketable, of course; something that is liquid. So more and more stocks are sold, which drives the price of each share down all the more. After all, there are many more sellers than buyers in this kind of market.

Also during this period, the price of houses drops dramatically, because if thousands cannot afford to make their mortgage payments, they are going to try to sell their homes. But who will want to buy a house, when mortgage rates are over 20%? Who can afford to carry a large mortgage at those rates? In southwestern Ontario, especially in Toronto, when the price of houses and rental offices dropped through the floor (and the basement as well), fortunes were lost, and many real estate companies were wiped out.

That's the scenario at the first part of the investment cycle, and it's not pretty. A common phrase used to describe this part of the market cycle is recession. As you know, recession can be very mild and short lived or it can prove to be truly awful and last for years. The worst-case scenario is called depression, when purchasing power and value actually erode. We have frequently heard of the Great Depression that existed from 1929 into the 1930s, when President Franklin Delano Roosevelt in the United States set up the Tennessee Valley Authority. The U.S. economy was in dire straits, no one was spending, and companies were dropping like flies. Things were so awful, that Roosevelt found himself declaring, "We've got to get Americans back to work! We have to spend our way out!"

Which is what they did, conceiving a whole new philosophy: deficit financing. (More on that below.) The federal government recognized that it needed a dam down in Tennessee, so it hired many thousands of Americans to build that dam. Then the government started building countless interstate highways to criss-cross the country, putting tens of thousands more citizens back to work.

When Americans returned home from their newly created jobs, they found that they had fixed that old 1926 Ford so often, they just couldn't fix it any more. So they purchased a new car. Then they got tired of fixing the washing machine . . .

The Government's Options — and the Model A Ford

Following President Roosevelt's example, many countries came to believe that the only way to get out of a deep recession was to spend your way out. North America saw, only a few short years ago, President Reagan and Prime Minister Trudeau using this old concept of deficit financing. When each country found itself doing poorly on the economic front, its government would promptly start spending like a drunken sailor, handing out contracts by the thousands to put its citizens back to work, turn things around, and "get the country working again."

This mentality explains to a large degree why we were in the situation we found ourselves in until very recently — with huge debts — and why both President Clinton and

Prime Minister Chrétien have shifted "to the middle" with their respective cutbacks in government spending, and their reluctance to begin new, expensive, make-work programs.

Another "cure" that federal governments often reach for in bad or difficult economic times is lower interest rates. When I think of these, an image of the Model A Ford comes to mind.

If you never had the pleasure of driving a Model A, ask your parents or grandparents. When you sat in the Model A Ford and pushed your foot on the accelerator right down to the floor, if the car didn't stall, something interesting happened: *Absolutely nothing!* It took a few seconds for the acceleration to kick in — and then, slowly, the vehicle would start to pick up speed.

The same is true with interest rates. When the government, because of its fiscal policy, reduces interest rates a little (to try to reduce the borrowing costs for itself and the public), in the hope of encouraging or even stimulating the economy, nothing (usually) happens immediately. After all, if interest rates drop, you may still be worried about where you are going to find a job — or if you will be able to keep the one you now have.

If the interest rates have been lowered by the various central banks of a government, what happens? The cost of servicing your debts goes down. And the public responds accordingly by taking any extra, newly disposable income to pay off its debts.

How does this help the economy? Not a bit. This action is simply meant to help individual situations. True, lowering interest rates will help over the long term, but never forget my example of the old Model A Ford: It will take a while to "get up to speed."

Generally speaking, when interest rates become lower, it takes nearly a year for the change to work its way through the economy until its most beneficial effects are felt.

A third option for governments is to focus on monetary policy: they can simply print more money. When the amount of money in circulation is increased, banks have greater access to more money, since their own borrowing rates are lower. The banks are more eager to lend money, which starts improving the situation.

So there you have the three basic solutions to a difficult economic situation: increase government spending, lower interest rates, or print more money.

Interest Rates are Falling — So Look at Bonds

Now, back to our diagram. As you slowly work your way down from twelve o'clock to three o'clock, you will notice that interest rates are slowly starting to drop. Where should you be investing now?

You might not want to invest in equities. The companies aren't making any money yet, so, although in the long term it's probably a good idea to invest in equities, most people will not. They are too unsure about how long it will take those stocks to start turning upward in price. (The really knowledgeable investors realize that this is the best time to grab those low-priced stocks. These folk are not called "contrarians" for nothing.)

A good investment is probably a GIC, because you can lock in that interest rate. But there is a better investment, and that is the bond. When you purchase a bond, you lock in those rates — for up to twenty-five years.

Bonds have two components worthy of note: They have the interest rate they pay out, and they have the value of the bond itself. A bond is different from a GIC in many ways. On a GIC (or term deposit, or Guaranteed Investment Certificate), the principal is 100% guaranteed, as is the interest rate until maturity. They are not liquid between the time of purchase and their maturity.

HOW BONDS WORK

Value of Bond

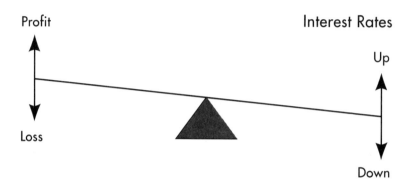

With a bond, the interest is fully guaranteed, but the principal is not guaranteed until maturity. So the value of the bond can actually fluctuate between the purchase date and maturity. (In a CSB, or Canada Savings Bond, the interest rate is guaranteed, usually for a year at a time, *and* the principal is 100% guaranteed — but the interest rate on the CSB will often have a minimum to which it can be reduced. When I refer to bonds, I am talking about non-CSB bonds, that is government bonds or provincial or corporate bonds.)

Let's look at how a bond works. Refer to the diagram above, as we will be discussing it in detail. You see what looks like a teeter-totter, which is, in fact, what it is. How do teeter-totters work? It's very simple. A teeter-totter is just a plank of wood supported in the exact middle by a fulcrum. Kids love to play on them. The further one child moves from the centre towards the end of the plank, the higher a child on the opposite end will be lifted in the air and the greater the thrill. The thrill is the result of the upwards and downwards movement of the teeter-totter as each child pushes himself off the ground, forcing the other child down to the ground.

Take a pencil or a pen and hold it in the middle. Assume

that on the right side of the pen, you have interest rates going up and down. On the left side of the pen, you have the value of a bond, which can also fluctuate up and down.

If you push the right side of the pen down (that is, interest rates go down), what happens to the left side of the pen? It goes up: As interest rates decrease, the value of your bond increases. This can also be called a capital gain.

The reverse works as well. When the right side of the pen is pushed up, the left side goes down. Therefore, as interest rates go up, the value of the bond goes down. If you sell the bond before maturity at a higher market interest rate than you purchased it at, you would have a capital loss.

Observe that the closer to the end of a teeter-totter you get, the greater the movement. With the bond, the greater or longer the maturity of the bond you hold, the greater the impact a small movement in interest rates will have on the value of the bond.

When the pen is parallel to the ground — or level — the interest rate is at the same rate as the bond you invested in. How much profit have you made on the fund now? At this point, you have made only the yearly interest-rate yield. You have not experienced any capital gain or loss, as reflected by the left side of the pen.

Here is a general rule (without specific numbers, because one needs a rather complicated computer program to work those out): On a ten-year bond, for every 1% that interest rates go down, a bond increases by about 6%. And a 2% drop in interest rates will average about a 12% increase on a bond.

Remember — this has nothing to do with the interest rate you are earning! This is the bond increasing in value, just as a stock increases in value as the price goes up.

So, at the top of the cycle, what would be a favourable place to invest, looking at risk versus reward? Definitely a guaranteed bond, because you would lock in the high interest rates. If interest rates were to drop, say 3%, you would ultimately make about 18% profit, plus the interest-rate yield each year! Not bad.

Let's look at an example: Assume that the interest rate goes down one full percent. If you had invested $10,000 in a GIC for one year and it was earning 10%, you would have made $1,000 in interest. If you were in the top tax bracket (assume 50%), $500 of that would go to pay tax, and you would be left with $500 to spend.

If you had the same $10,000 in a bond, which was paying the same 10%, you would make the same $1,000 in interest over the course of a year. Naturally, you would have to pay the same $500 in income tax, so you would be left with $500 — exactly the same as your GIC. But remember — bonds have that other, rather interesting component (don't forget the teeter-totter image). When interest rates drop 1% on a ten-year bond, you receive about a 6% capital gain if you sell the bond, or an extra $600 from the $10,000 you invested. A capital gain is the increase in the value of an asset and is triggered only if the asset is sold. Capital gains are given preferential tax treatment. Twenty-five percent of a capital gain earned is tax free — in this case, $150 is tax-free, with the remaining $450 taxable at your top marginal tax bracket.

What's happened here? You must pay $225 in tax, leaving you with $225 after tax — plus the $150 that you received tax free. Now you have $375 after tax — plus you have the interest that you earned on the bond! So, you have $875 spendable from that bond, as opposed to a mere $500 from your investment in a GIC! (In both cases, you still have your $10,000 initial investment.)

A bond is a 100% guaranteed investment; if you hold it to maturity, you are guaranteed to get your initial investment back. The only risk comes if you choose to cash it out in the interim, which is where the teeter-totter comes into play. If you are a conservative investor, you have locked into a fully-guaranteed investment that has the potential to increase in value if interest rates drop! Risk? Assuming the government of Canada is going to be around for the next few decades at least, and you purchase a bond backed by our federal government, there is practically zero risk, since it is guaranteed. At this point in the cycle, bonds make excellent investments.

Turn back to the diagram on p. 38. You can see that just after twelve o'clock would be the best time to invest in bonds, at the point when the interest rates start to drop.

Twelve O'clock to Three O'clock: Interest Rates Head South

When interest rates start to drop, most Canadians tend to pay down their highest interest-rate debt — their credit cards. Once they pay off some of those brutally interest-ridden Visa, Master-Card, and American Express balances, they usually like to put a bit of money in the bank for an emergency cash reserve.

With interest rates falling, you've been slowly paying off your debts, and beginning to accumulate a bit of money. Don't forget, though, that interest rates may remain relatively high for a while, so you may still keep the tattered sofa, the aging automobile, and the not-very-efficient washing machine.

But most consumers reach a point where they say — feeling fairly confident that they'll keep their job — "Let's bite the bullet, darling, and buy something!" Smart move, since a lot of business owners who have been tripping over their slow-moving inventory for a while now have decided that it's better to stay in business than to go belly-up. So quite a few retailers are having sales of 40%, even 50%, off.

People with cash do incredibly well at these times, when goods are at their absolute cheapest. ("Look, sweetie, that washing machine is 70% off — it's almost at cost or below cost!") But the manufacturers just want to keep their plants open; they want to be able to survive. They know that these things go in cycles, and they want to stay in business, so they are chopping their prices as low as they can, while still staying alive.

How about housing? Quite often, the people who are constructing houses — the builders — are giving low interest rates at these times. So instead of a two-year interest rate of 10% on your mortgage, you will get it for a lot less.

Everybody is giving as deep a discount as they possibly can, to encourage people to spend money. And as you and your fellow Canadians slowly start to spend your money, the employers finally begin to get rid of their inventory build-up. Of course, if you were an employer, and you'd just struggled through a rough year where interest rates were high and you had nearly lost your business, would you run out and hire a few dozen new workers, when things were *just beginning* to get back on track?

Probably not.

What you might do, however, would be to give some overtime to several workers. Or you might bring in a few new part-timers since, if they work less than three or four hours a day, you don't have to pay Canada Pension on their behalf. And if you are working at that plant — and you can see that orders are picking up a bit and part-timers are being hired — how would you feel about your job and its prospects *now*?

You would feel a little better, I sense, so maybe you would be more inclined to spend a little bit of money for a change. It may be as minor as taking the spouse and/or kids out to dinner, or you might take that brief vacation you cancelled last year or finally replace that old 14-inch TV.

It is a long process, but things do slowly start turning around in the economy. And more and more companies (finally) start to break even, maybe even start to make a little profit.

THREE O'CLOCK TO SIX O'CLOCK: (ALMOST) EVERYONE IS HAPPY

We are now at about three o'clock in the investment cycle. At this time, you would be wise to look at buying equity investments. There's no guarantee that the shares of most companies will start to do well immediately, but they are starting to turn the corner; this is when you might consider speaking with your investment advisor. "When there is blood in the streets," to paraphrase the great father of the Templeton fund, "that's when you want to start investing in equities."

What if you are a conservative investor? Remember that bonds are still going to do well, at least until the clock strikes six o'clock, which represents the bottoming out of interest rates. At this point you might want to start adding to your equity position, but *not* necessarily choosing to sell your bonds. Over the long term, if you look strictly at the statistics, you will do better in a "straight equity investment" than you will "in bonds alone." That is a categorical truth — the numbers always show it to be correct. Even as a conservative investor, you may want to consider beginning to move more money into equities. Meanwhile, the government continues to lower interest rates a bit, and the economy is starting to pick up and look better.

The interest rates continue to go down. Who is happy now? Anybody with loans. Business owners. Real estate salespeople. Much of the general public.

Who is starting to get less and less happy? Those seniors who are on a fixed income, because they weren't brave or adventurous enough to put money into equities or bonds. As their GICs or term deposits are coming due, they usually are not informed enough to buy bonds, because nobody has explained the cycle to them. Instead, they renew those high-interest-yielding GICs at significantly lower rates. Their income is going to drop, probably precipitously.

Things continue to go well for everyone else. The stock market starts to improve and interest rates continue to drop until we reach six o'clock, which corresponds to the lowest point of the interest rates. Who is happy now, and what does the world look like at this point?

Investors are happy again, since they can borrow cheaply and invest pretty successfully. The stock market is flourishing.

People's debts are starting to go up again. The economy is chugging along. Everyone is happy!

Well, not *everyone*, in fact. Those poor seniors again! Now that GIC rates are at an all-time low, their income from those certificates has dropped greatly. They don't have nearly as much to spend, whether on the grandchildren, on that usual trip to Florida, or even on their own rent. As a result, they start to complain.

On a supply-and-demand basis, what has happened? The money supply is quite liberal, so there's lots of cash floating around; interest rates are low, so demand for new products is higher than it has been in years; but supplies of many things are starting to get low, because there is this huge, ever-growing demand! There is a lot of money chasing what has become too few goods.

At this point in the investment cycle, you don't see sales of 50% off; they're more likely at 10% or 15% off, if even that. The economic situation is starting to look different. And the government begins to look closer at the overall picture again.

How about housing, for example? Housing starts, which really began when the clock was at three or four o'clock, are now at all-time highs. When you hear about "major improvement in housing starts!" in the news, what does it mean?

It means plenty. After all, a house is usually the biggest purchase the average Canadian makes in his or her life. As a result, it is very, very interest-rate sensitive, and as soon as people see an opening, they don't usually want to rent anymore. They are well aware that when they rent, they are just giving money to somebody else, every single month, and getting no equity from it. They want to own something. Most of us want a nest, a place to call our own.

And let us not forget, when you purchase a new or used house, you're not buying only a house. You have to buy drapes, lots of paint, a lawnmower, a vacuum cleaner. When you rented, throwing up a poster on that blank wall was probably acceptable to you. (Indeed, the landlord may well have had rules against hammering nails into those holy walls.) But now you own a home — a reflection of you, a part of you — and a blank wall, or a pasted-up poster, is no longer good enough. You have to own a painting of some kind, or a print, or an artistic plate. You start spending.

It's also important to recall that when a house is built, there are many hundreds of person-hours involved. Think of all the people it takes to put a house up, not to mention the materials, bricks, nails, plumbing, paint, wood, the spin-off businesses — you name it. And there's more. The more houses there are, the more natural gas is consumed, since it's piped into the house. The more water, the more sewage — and the more government employees who must build those pipes, those sewers. Spin-offs, indeed. That is why economists are always talking about "housing starts" — they affect just about every industry there is.

At this point in the economic cycle, everyone is happy again — except those poor seniors, who are on a fixed budget.

FROM SIX O'CLOCK TO NINE O'CLOCK: NEW WORRIES, NEW CONCERNS

Now we start hearing about "inflation fears," when the government warns that inflation has begun to pick up. Uh-oh! If we're not careful, the economy will get overheated — and let's not forget that the economy is like that old Model A Ford: if the driver takes his foot off the accelerator, does the vehicle start to slow down immediately? Absolutely not. It doesn't have the gear ratio that today's cars possess. It just keeps barrelling down the highway.

So what does the government do? It slowly starts to raise interest rates — bit by bit. Now, if you own a bond, remember that the point of maximum profit or capital gains is when interest rates have bottomed out. When interest rates are rising, the longer you hold that bond, the greater the loss of the capital gains you had built up. True, you will still get the guaranteed interest rate, but from this point on, bonds are just not as attractive as they were before. After all, if you hold on to them, you will be giving away profit that is already in your pocket. If you are thinking of purchasing a bond, it should be a short-term bond when interest rates are low, so there will be very low, if any, capital losses.

This is the point where people who like to try to "time the bond market" are getting out of bonds. But equities are still good, because with interest rates so low, and the economy doing well, corporations begin to raise their prices, due to the demand/supply ratio. "Let's make some profit," they think; they remember the lean years. And what happens to stock prices? They go up, and millions of people make a lot of money in the stock market, if they choose carefully and purchase quality companies. People are feeling more confident. There are a lot of jobs available. Unemployment figures are low.

Yes — you guessed it: The government starts tightening the screws more and more. At first, that has very little effect, but as we move towards nine o'clock, and the interest rates go up, people start spending less. As they spend less, corporate profits start to be reduced a little bit, so the stock market begins to get pretty volatile. (One month the market may do well; the next month, it is dropping rapidly. Ring a bell?)

There is a huge focus now on the profitability of stocks. "How well are they doing?" everyone asks. In reality, it is still a good time to be in the market — but people are starting to question the wisdom of staying in. At some point, and this varies from individual to individual, the interest rates rise to a level where people say to themselves, "You know, maybe we should just repair the old junk heap rather than purchase a new one." There are few sales going on in your friendly neighbourhood mall.

This is a period of maximum profit. Slowly, people start to back off from spending. "You know, dear, the interest rates are up quite a bit; are you sure we can afford this thing? Maybe we should just wait a little bit longer."

What happens, of course, is that demand slowly starts to drop. At first, this has very little effect on business. And who is happy now? Surprise — the seniors are happy, at least a bit, because their interest rates are going up, so their fixed income is rising, and they have more money to spend than before. Businesses are still making a profit too, which is welcome — but their inventory levels begin to creep up. And the time, at the sound of the beep, is nine o'clock.

Interest rates have been increasing at various points during this period, and the stock market isn't doing so well anymore because people aren't purchasing as many goods, thereby making the profits of many of the corporations begin to fall. Profits haven't stopped, of course; remember, we're not at twelve o'clock, which represents the peak of interest rates, so it's not a massive recession. But public consumption is slowing down, corporate profits are down, and the stock market, like a cat on a hot tin roof, is looking increasingly edgy and tense.

At this moment, you can look back and see that stocks have had their major run — from three to nine o'clock. So what is left? If stocks are now not doing very well, recall that teeter-totter: If interest rates are still rising, are bonds a good place to be invested?

Probably not, because as they go up, you will probably lose.

How about GICs? Do you want to lock your money into a long-term GIC?

Absolutely not! If interest rates are still going up, why on earth would you want to lock in at 6% or 7%? A year from now, the rate could be at 8%, even 9%!

So the best place to go is short. Go into money market, T-bills, and wait until interest rates get back to the top — when we begin the cycle at twelve o'clock again.

OF COURSE, THINGS CAN CHANGE THAT CYCLE A BIT

That is the general investment cycle and how it works. An average cycle lasts between five and seven years, but this varies, of course. (If we knew exactly how long each cycle lasted to the day, month, or even year, we'd all be rich from forecasting it and taking advantage of its rises and falls!)

There are countless things that can cause that investment cycle to change. For example, at the end of 1997 into early 1998, we were at a period where we sort of levelled off at six o'clock — interest rates had risen a bit, and people were starting to talk about "inflation coming again."

And then what happened? The Asian-Contagion, Asian Flu, whatever you want to call it. Asia simply crashed, and major markets in the Far East shook to their very core. It was an awful experience for many countries in the Far East and hard on many mutual funds and investors who "had money in Asia."

It isn't hard to see why, when Asia sneezes, Canada could catch pneumonia: Resources, from coal to oil to silver to wood products, account for some 40% of our exports. And Asia is one of the largest consumers of raw materials in the world. All of a sudden — bang! — we should have been reaching the part in the investment cycle that causes everything to accelerate. Interest rates should have gone up, but instead it was like somebody threw ice-cold water on everything!

Suddenly, almost overnight, a major portion of the world and its economy, one that accounted for a huge demand for Canadian goods, was cutting off that demand! This caused many investment managers to make far less than they usually would, because, generally speaking, in the hours between six o'clock and nine o'clock — when there are huge demands for products — the price of raw materials usually rises. So one would expect resource funds to do well. After all, if everybody around the world is consuming a lot of resources, the price of these funds understandably rises. But no — early in 1998, resources were hammered, as were the mutual funds that invested in them and the stocks of the companies that discover, refine, and sell them.

In early 1998, when we should have been moving to the end of the bull market cycle, the demand from Asia dropped off, the demand/supply curve started to flatten out, and inflation became less of a problem. The demand from Asia ceased, which slowed the economy down, causing the market cycle to last for a longer than average period of time.

Money managers who ordinarily moved into resources at that time found themselves losing 20% to 30% on their investments over a short period.

Now, as we enter the new millennium, Asia has recovered nicely. The price of many raw materials has increased, which has helped some oil companies' shares to rebound. The United States has been, and continues to be, the engine that fuels world growth. Interest rates have risen a bit, but inflation still looks to be a non-issue. It's amazing how much things can change in just a short period!

My point: The market cycle is never truly fixed. The timing can be thrown off. Many things can abruptly enter the picture and skew it, especially with the planet shrinking courtesy of communications technology, and every country becoming truly interdependent.

Still, I hope this chapter gave you a good idea of how the investment cycle goes: When interest rates reach a peak, everybody and everything slows down; nobody is buying, inflation is high, and the cycle starts all over again.

That is why a lot of investment advisors who follow philosophies such as Warren Buffet's buy-and-hold (as reflected in Infinity Mutual Funds, see Chapter Seven), insist that the facts, and the Money Gods, are on their side: There is no possible way of timing the market successfully. They insist — and who am I to argue? — that nobody knows exactly when things are going to happen, in the market, in Asia, in the world, in life.

Looking through a rear-view mirror, it all looks logical, but when you are involved in it, as we all must be, you simply cannot tell for sure. It wasn't by chance that the brilliant media critic Marshall McLuhan noted wittily, "We don't know who discovered water, but it probably wasn't a fish." Translation: Fish are too busy, swimming about in H_2O to be able to name it or understand it or even imagine it. So, too, with the investment cycle: When we are caught up in it, we never know for sure whether it is three, six, nine, or even twelve o'clock, or whether the time will shift back and forth several hours, much less when it might do so.

One result of all this volatility is that stocks held for the long term tend to give you the greatest return. That is why a lot of financial advisors suggest that you buy stocks — quality stocks — and hold them for a long, long time. And that is one of the best philosophies around in the world of investing.

But if you understand how the investment cycle works — and I hope this chapter has helped — and you don't want to be fully invested in equities (and only equities), you can develop the ability to skew your portfolio slightly towards bonds when the "market timing" is appropriate. And maybe, just maybe, you will increase your cash component when that is appropriate, as well.

CHAPTER FIVE

Some Thoughts
on Demographics

In the previous chapter, I tried to give you an understanding of the market in general, and of the sequence of events that usually unfolds every market cycle. A major consideration you ought to be aware of when you invest is the question of demographics.

Why is this important? Because demographics shape the way in which many events occur. They always have and they always will. In the second half of the 1990s, several excellent books looked at this subject, from *Boom, Bust & Echo* to *The Pig and the Python*. The title of the latter gives a strong image to what demographics mean, in terms of the market.

A python stretched out in a long, straight line would represent normal demographics. Now imagine a large lump — the swallowed pig — as it works its way through the body of the python. This represents what is happening to the marketplace at the turn of the millennium, as the baby boomers increase in age.

Imagine far more 20-year-olds in our society. Then imagine far more 30-year-olds. Then more 40-year-olds. As the boomers move from one demographic into the next, they vastly swell the normal ranks of people in each decade, which creates significantly more demand for age-sensitive products and services and hence, more opportunity for the corporations that sell these products and services.

Learning from history and projecting this knowledge into the future, an industry can place itself in a position where it can benefit from this huge wave of people. A simple, clear example would be Gerber, the baby food people. After the Second World War came to an end, and veterans flocked back to their homes around the world by the millions, the number of births increased substantially. What happened to the demand for baby food during those post-war years? It shot up incredibly. And, understandably, so did the price of the common shares of Gerber on the stock market. What happened to the number of diapers that were manufactured? They increased with demand, too. And the companies that produced diapers — first cloth, then disposable — made a great deal of money, as did those who invested in them.

Later, when the average baby boomer first reached school age, what happened? There was an insufficient number of schools, so more had to be built — whether kindergartens, lower schools, or junior or high schools. You would have thought that boards of education would have seen what was happening in junior highs and started building more high schools. And that men and women in the world of post-secondary education would have noted the explosion on the high school level and built more universities.

This did not happen. Every time these pig-in-the-python movements took place, the school systems were caught off guard, and a massive number of schools were quickly built. When you look at most schools across North America today, you see new trailers and countless "portables" that have been placed on playgrounds, next to permanent buildings, to try to cope with the huge number of students going to school.

And speaking of demographics, look at all those universities that were built over the past few decades. Today, many of these institutions of higher learning are complaining about funding. They never seem to have enough money to sustain what they already have and/or what they need to grow. It's clear that they need more support than they are now receiving. However, now that the baby boomers have passed through university, it's understandable that there is less demand for higher education than there was right after the Second World War (for the returning veterans), and throughout the 1960s and early 1970s.

What happened then? The baby boomers got married. And what was the first giant purchase most of them made? A house. Recall how real estate demand and prices soared through the 1970s and into the 1980s. It made sense, really; this seemingly endless supply of baby boomers was creating an enormous demand for housing. There were not enough houses for them, so more and more houses had to be constructed. And because these new houses could not be built fast enough, the price skyrocketed.

As all these millions of baby boomers continued to age, what happened subsequently to the price of housing? Naturally, it dropped a little, because the builders kept on building all of these houses, and with the demand subsiding, house prices began to fall.

You can see the opportunity that an understanding of demographics provides, when you take the time to look at what the average 20-year-old does, and the average 30-, 40-, 50-, and 60-year-old. Furthermore, when you realize that the number of people in each of those decades can often explode (as it did with the soldiers returning home after the Second World War, marrying, and starting to raise families), this creates tremendous opportunity!

I believe that *Boom, Bust & Echo*, written by David K. Foot and Daniel Stoffman, published by Macfarlane, Walter & Ross of Toronto (and its update, *Boom, Bust & Echo 2000*), should be compulsory reading for every Canadian. Of particular importance is the first chapter, which illustrates how the year in which you were born has affected your opportunities.

What's This Got To Do with Investments?

There is an old expression that goes something like, "Sure, sure, sure — but what's this got to do with the price of eggs?" Well, this book is about investing and investments, so let me cut to the chase: How does this awareness of the power of ever-changing demographics affect the world of investing?

Plenty. If you talk with the average baby boomer — and they have been turning 50 at the rate of over a half-dozen every minute, for the past few years — I think you will hear most of them say, "I don't believe the government will support me and my family in the way it supported my parents in the past." Most boomers feel that the Canada Pension Plan, never mind the Old Age Supplement/Seniors Benefit, will not be around long enough to provide for their own retirement years.

If I am correct, several million Canadian baby boomers are saving for their retirements. But where are they going to put their money?

They clearly have a choice: They can invest in equities, GICs, bonds, real estate, or other types of investments. It's been clearly proven that you do not make money, after taxes and inflation, investing in GICs over the long term. GICs can be good for short-term savings, but over the long term, they are simply not a good investment. Since most baby boomers tend to be better educated than their parents (because so many of that earlier generation made darned sure their children had access to higher education), most of the boomers' money is not going into GICs.

Where is it going? A very popular investment has been mutual funds. When I started in the business of financial planning in 1986, I had to explain to people what these "mutual funds" were. A good number of people had not heard of them, or if they had, they were unaware of how they worked.

Many would become interested, and go to their bank and say, "I want to take X amount of money from my GICs and move it into mutual funds." And many bankers exclaimed in horror, "Do you have any idea what you are doing? These things aren't guaranteed! You could lose all your money! Are you willing to take risks like that?"

How times have changed. Today, when you approach your friendly neighbourhood banker, he or she will probably announce, "We have all these mutual funds of our own to offer! Here are the no-loads I can recommend! The management fee is . . ."

It's really quite amazing how, in a brief ten-year period, mutual funds went from being "dubious" and "risky" investments, to something the average bank manager eagerly and enthusiastically markets! This is a remarkable change.

What caused this changing response to mutual funds? You guessed it — the baby boomers, who are so eager to invest because they do not believe that the federal government will take care of them in their declining years. As a result, billions upon billions of dollars every year have been thrown into the only asset class that, over the long term, has consistently made money: equities. But because straight purchases of stocks still frighten many (a fear not helped by the Bre-Xs and the Livents of the second half of the 1990s), the boomers have chosen to invest in equities through "the far safer" vehicle of mutual funds.

If you pop into a library or use the Internet to check out any newspaper of a half-dozen years ago, you may be surprised at how few mutual funds were being offered and listed in the business section. Look at it today, as we move towards the millennium! Many Canadian newspapers didn't even have business sections a decade ago; today, major sections and even entire newspapers are dedicated to the subject. Baby boomers have an unquenchable thirst for knowledge about investments and investing.

What does this desire to invest money mean on a large scale? In its simplest terms, it means that you have a large number of people demanding equities, with a limited supply of equities being offered. Over most of the decade of the 1990s, we have seen what then occurs: Stock prices move up and up and up. North America was very bullish throughout the decade, and it still appears to be, even after the scary, volatile summer and fall of 1998. Most people feel that equities (and the mutual funds that buy them by the millions) will continue to do astoundingly well over the next ten, maybe even fifteen years.

A few years ago, I was at a conference about the world of investing. And although I do not recall the name of the professor who said the following words, what he said has stuck to me like glue: "If you are not invested in the equity market over the next fifteen years, not only will you be disappointed; your children will be disappointed; and their children will be disappointed as well."

What we've been witnessing over the past decade has been one of the greatest creations of wealth in human history — all because of supply and demand. Imagine if you could zap yourself in a time machine back into the 1970s in any major Canadian city. In that decade, it was almost impossible to not make money in real estate!

It didn't last forever, but great fortunes were made during those years. I have a friend who bought a home in mid-town Toronto in 1971, not as an investment, but as a place to live and start his family. He paid $41,000 for it. By 1973, it was worth over $100,000; by 1975, it was worth $200,000; by 1980, it was worth nearly half a million. (And it wasn't a particularly large or attractive house, either.) Just by owning this little piece of property through that decade, this fellow saw his original real estate purchase shoot up over 1,000%.

The baby boomers clearly chose the world of mutuals to deposit their billions, and it's pretty clear that as they retire in the first decade or two of the twenty-first century, they will continue to be comfortable with that kind of investment. They will, in many cases, set up Systematic Withdrawal Plans (SWPs — see Chapter Ten) as well, and/or take out various kinds of income streams from those investments.

All this investing has helped make Canada (and the other nations in which you may have been investing) exceptionally strong. And the reason behind this is enlightening. Canada used to be known as a source of funds for people from other countries. They could come to this country and borrow money from the Canadian banks and use it to purchase Canadian businesses. Then, in turn, they would take their profits out of Canada in the form of dividends.

This not-very-pleasant system kept Canada relatively poor, as profits from our corporations were sent elsewhere around the world. This does not happen any longer. Over the past few years, baby boomers have been buying all those equities, especially international ones. We are now taking the profits from those firms, both Canadian and worldwide. Understandably, when we take profits out of European companies and bring them to Canada, it increases the net worth of this country, which, in turn, makes Canada astonishingly wealthy.

Over the long term, Canada clearly has a debt problem, and it's very important that we deal with that problem, preferably within this generation. (Of course, the baby boomers will trigger billions of dollars of income tax when they die.) What you have is a generation that has been accumulating a massive amount of wealth in their investments in equities, and upon their death, what's left after their expenditures will be taxable.

Clearly, the Canadian government is depending upon this huge transfer of wealth in order to pay down the overwhelming debts it has created over the past decades. The question is, can the feds continue their recent resolve, or will they return to the unfortunate tradition of passing these towering debts onto future generations?

In the meanwhile, Canadians have one of the highest

marginal tax rates in the world, which makes it very difficult for Canadian entrepreneurs to compete. These men and women can simply cross the border into the United States, where the taxes are significantly lower. There is a free flow of talent across the 49th parallel, which is something that Canada should be very concerned about. Brain drains can create a real dilemma. We depend on a knowledgeable portion of our population to build companies and create wealth, but if the environment isn't profitable, many of our finest entrepreneurs, scholars, and scientists will simply leave our country. It's a type of resource which we cannot afford to lose. And we have been losing plenty.

In 1986, there were 10,000 Canadians enrolled in American universities, studying engineering, sciences, or business. Today about 23,000 Canadian students attend American universities. Nearly 800,000 native-born Canadians live in the United States. This number does not include snow birds, those with temporary work permits, and illegal aliens.

An interesting note to consider is that the U.S. Department of Commerce statistics show that Canadian immigrants are the most educated of all. It's the highly trained, wealthy, and entrepreneurial Canadians who are leaving our country.

WHY YOU MUST KEEP YOUR
EYE ON THE DEMOGRAPHIC BALL

The above discussion provides the key to understanding the significance of demographics to investing. Certain areas of the market should outperform others as the boomers take advantage of or are using services or products provided by companies or industries.

Technology is one such industry. Think of the number of computers that existed a decade ago, and the number that are used (and have become essential) today. Our ancestors passed through the Industrial Revolution, and we are clearly going through a High-Technology Revolution today, which has led to our era being labelled the Information Age. Many — but not all — companies that are involved in the computer area will have a very positive outlook, because that is clearly where the momentum is.

And how about health care? One need not have a doctorate in demography to note that our population is aging at a rate unheard of in recorded history. Whether it is hospitals or pharmaceutical companies or health care products, anything that is catering to our aging population probably has a strong future and can look forward to a steady increase in stock price.

The trick, then, is to know the services that the baby boomers (turning 50 every few seconds, remember!) are going to be requiring or demanding. Travel, for example. Do you recall that the cruise lines and cruise ships back in the early 1990s were in deep trouble? Today at the end of that same decade, they are making massive profits, earning money hand over fist, building new ships and cruising everywhere except in outer space. Why? Because a cruise is a very convenient, we'll-take-care-of-all-your-needs sort of vacation, and our aging boomers have been gravitating towards it like never before.

What you must do, of course, when you are investing for the long term — especially if you are implementing an SWP strategy, or something else in which you do not wish to shift your assets around a lot — is to be sure that you have your money in a growth industry, as opposed to a declining industry. An example of the latter would be the world of resources. Most of the resources on this earth have been found. What you are talking about when you discuss resources is a very cyclical industry that is ultimately in decline. Why would anyone wish to commit large sums of money to that area, especially for the long term? For the short term, it could definitely make sense. (Indeed, there were a few years around 1990 when resource stocks and mutual funds were doing magnificently.) But over the long term, oil reserves are slowly dwindling, and the larger oil companies have already sold off their huge blocks of land to the smaller producers that have better efficiencies; it looks like a declining industry. (People will continue to play in resource stocks and mutual funds, and there can definitely be money made in the future, but over the long term, a growth industry is the way to go.) The future is not in non-renewable, environmentally destructive fossil fuels. The future lies in more friendly, yet-to-be-discovered-or-perfected alternatives.

You should purchase your investments when the entire industry you are interested in is growing at a fast rate. Why? Because the ground swell of its movement will mean that, although you may experience periods of stock market losses, overall the trend should be upward. It's a given that it's far easier to find successful investments in growth areas and industries. Ones to consider are clearly technology, health care, and telecommunications.

DEMOGRAPHICS AREN'T THAT HARD TO FOLLOW!

Watch the commercials on television, as they change over the years: They tend to suggest our wants (if not our needs!). In spite of that, I hardly think we should choose our goals based on what some crackerjack salesman or advertising guru in Toronto, New York, or California suggests. But we might get some pretty good ideas of where to put our hard-earned money if we are more sensitive to those advertisements we are bombarded with every day!

Be aware of the real-life demographics when you are visiting the local shopping centre or the neighbourhood mall. What's everyone buying? What are the new trends? If you like to golf, think about Callaway, the golf equipment company, for a moment. It seems that over the last few years, nearly every golfer had Callaway clubs. Then their competitor, Titalist, was "in." Soon golfers had moved on to yet another, True Lie clubs. These are the types of opportunities you can see around you that are obviously influenced by demographics. They all have one thing in common: the classic, ancient, Scottish game of golf. When you ask yourself why golf is so popular, the answer is soon clear: Baby boomers are more concerned with their health. They are more athletic. They have more disposable time and money. They like getting out. Golf is a very social event.

You could make a similar argument about the health care area. If you look around you and see your parents aging — even see yourself aging! — you might want to place some of your more "aggressive" money in that area.

As you can see, a sensitivity to demographics can go a long way to improving your financial future. Keep your eye on the ball, watch those eternal commercials with a curious, not glazed eye, and remember that big, fat pig making its way through the hungry python. In those images, a much happier retirement lies.

Chapter Six

The Decade Game

Each of us likes to think of ourselves as a unique individual, separate from the masses. And, of course, we are. But there are patterns that do exist. We tend to follow a kind of herding instinct, and we tend to do things that are similar to what others in our generation do.

In this chapter I'd like to take a little time to look at the various generations — decades, really — and see some of the things they have in common, as well as some of the pitfalls they all encounter. My purpose should be obvious: If we can see similarities between ourselves and other people our age, maybe we can learn from them and get a few good, helpful investment ideas.

THE TUMULTUOUS 20s

When young people enter their 20s, they are usually recently out of high school or attending college or university. They may be renting a vehicle or may have recently purchased a new car. Their focus is on clothes and dating, and the last thing they are thinking about is the future. In a nutshell, this is a time of consumption. If these youngsters have been in post-secondary education for a while and have just graduated, they want to spend. As a result, people this age rarely think about saving.

This is a shame, of course, as I hope the rest of this book will make clear. If you put aside even a small sum of money when you are in your early 20s, that small sum could turn into a surprisingly and thrillingly large amount of money only a few decades later, thanks to the miracle of compounding interest (and a wise selection of quality stocks and mutual funds).

But history and demographics and human nature have shown us that the 20s are hardly a decade when very many people think about anything much beyond — well, beyond being in their 20s!

THE THOROUGHLY THRILLING 30s

By the time we reach our 30s, most of us are married, and the biggest single idea on our minds is usually purchasing a home.

By the age of 30, most are in the process of that major move, and many have already had children. Kids, you may be shocked to read, are very expensive. In December 1998, a report based on data from the National Longitudinal Survey of Children and Youth, along with other Statistics Canada surveys, stated that the cost of raising a child from birth to the age of 18 is $160,000, up $4,000 from 1995. The Canadian Council on Social Development noted that some $52,000 of this child-rearing budget goes towards child care; other items include shelter ($37,000); food ($30,000); clothing ($16,000); and recreation ($13,000). And that's for only one child — what if you choose to have two, three, or more?

Clearly, Canadian parents in their 30s go through an incredible change in their lifestyle when the Little People come along. Where they previously would go out to theatres or nice restaurants, suddenly most, if not all, disposable income now ends up being spent on such things as cute clothing outfits or the latest must-have toy for little Adam or Amanda.

This can be a very difficult stage for a lot of people. Why? Because quite often, their generation, which has had a "me" focus, suddenly moves from selfishness to a life focused on children. (If this shift does *not* take place, it quite often leads to marital tensions, because these future adults sure take up a lot of time — often 90% of it.)

Painful as it is to think about, our 30s are precisely the time when we should seriously be looking to at least starting to save. After all, most 30-year-olds, whether male or female, are probably in the work force.

The best way to save is dollar-cost averaging. This is just a fancy term for investing equal amounts of money over equal periods of time. (Monthly is a good period to choose.) If the market goes up, your money buys fewer shares for the amount of dollars going in. But if the market goes down, your money purchases a greater number of shares for your fixed contribution. Over time, this practice results in an averaging of the unit price of your investments. (Simple example: One month, you are buying mutual funds that sell for $10.00; the next month, they drop to $9.00. Your average unit price over those two months is $9.50.)

As long as you keep putting your money into good quality investments that have a solid prospect for long-term growth, you'll have a very good result. You have discovered the guaranteed way to "beat the market" — by averaging your cost over time.

This is also a decade when young men and women should be aiming to maximize their RRSPs. And, as I've suggested earlier, it is wise to save a little money outside the RRSP as well. Of course, there's a catch, as always: During this decade, for most people, cash flow is very difficult to contain; there's that mortgage and the constant need for new clothes or shoes for the kids. In addition, you have to keep up your own clothes and shoes for work, since you must maintain an appropriate appearance. (And with two spouses working, as has become the case in the vast majority of Canadian households, clothing becomes all the more costly.)

Usually, money is extremely short for most of us during this decade. However, it is absolutely critical that people start to save during this period of time — and this is why:

Let's say that by the age of 30 you have managed to save $10,000. (Congratulations; in reality, few manage to do this.) If you were able to manage a 12% annual return on that money — not an unreasonably optimistic amount, considering the quality of stocks and mutual funds available nowadays — *that money would double every six years.*

When you're 36, your original $10,000 investment, without any further additions, would have turned into $20,000. By 42, it would be $40,000. At age 48, you would have $80,000 invested. At 54, you would possess $160,000. At the age of 60, you would have $320,000 invested — and by the age of 66 — at about the time when most men and women are retiring from their regular jobs and incomes — you would have $640,000! (This is assuming the money compounds completely tax free — i.e., in an RRSP.)

Think about it: Nearly two-thirds of a million dollars, all from a single $10,000 investment made at the age of 30! When you're ready to use the money, that $640,000, set up under a Systematic Withdrawal Plan, would yield a $60,000-or-so income flow, every single year thereafter! Not bad, from a simple ten grand put away early in one's life.

I understand that this is not easy for many, probably the vast majority of people, at that age. The cost of the baby! The monthly hit of that mortgage! And now the car is on the fritz and the washing machine is broken again! Some advisors are becoming more realistic about the difficulties of saving at an early age, in effect saying, don't beat yourself up, 30-year-olds, you can't do it all. There will be enough time to save later. Give yourself a break and stop feeling guilty. They also acknowledge the loss of the compound interest effect, but realize it's just not possible for many families to do it all. This is where many a grandparent — if they have the money, of course — could help their children and grandchildren to a striking extent. As I love to say, "If you have a little bit of extra money to help out your children, it's always lovelier to give with a warm hand than with a cold one. And look at what that relatively small gift, if invested, can amount to, by the time your kids reach the age you are at now!"

Let me surprise you for a moment. Let's see what happens if you keep putting off saving that money. Say it took you six more years to collect $10,000 to invest; in other words, you are now 36 years of age when you truly begin to save. Most people would look at that statement and say, "Big deal. So you started saving a half-dozen years later! You've lost only ten grand in earnings."

But it really *is* a big deal. When you're 66, that initial "hesitation" of little over half a decade means that you would have achieved an investment of "only" $320,000, instead of $640,000! In other words, a difference of nearly one-third of a million bucks, in potential retirement income, by just waiting those six years!

These *are* the years when it's the most difficult to save. But unless you know your income will rise substantially (so that you can assume you'll be able to put away large chunks of money in the future), you will have to look to saving now. And *at the earliest age possible!*

THE FINANCIALLY FICKLE 40S

As men and women move into their 40s, they are at an age when they are approaching their maximum earning power. If you are a full-time employee or entrepreneur, you will probably find that your work demands more of your time than ever. You are probably working overtime to keep your job or increase your business.

This is a time in life when most of us either become real

successes in our chosen professions or we get side-lined. As a result, a lot of people become workaholics during this decade.

Forty-somethings associate more and more with those whom they wish to emulate. This often means befriending men and women who are in slightly higher stations than they are. As a result, it can seem important to have the right kind of car and to live in the right neighbourhood. Joining the right organization, getting a golf club membership — all these things probably never crossed your mind at earlier stages of your life when you were occupied in other ways.

You now have the ability to set yourself up for the rest of your life. This is the decade when you are cementing yourself into your position in life. And, generally speaking, people spend to get to that position and then spend to stay there.

There are pitfalls, of course. Most of us still chuckle about the so-called Yuppies, or Young Urban Professionals, who spent beyond their means throughout the 1980s. They spent everything they had and then lived on plastic — buying now and paying later. They usually carried credit card balances (which often had annual interest rates of 25% and more). They ate at the best restaurants, instead of brown-bagging it, and they were always out spending, spending, spending.

People in their 40s must remember that if they wish to retire by the age of 60, they have only two decades left to save. Even if you put money away in nice little lumps beginning at age 40, and even if it compounds at that pleasant 12% return, that money has the opportunity to double only three times before the person is 58. If you had invested $10,000 in your 40s, it would increase to $20,000 in six years (just as it did for the 30-year-old) and to $80,000 in eighteen years. But, by the age of 58 — when you may be looking at your chances of an early retirement — you may find that you have to keep working to get another six years of compounding so the money can increase sixteen-fold.

Notice how those "compounding years" have dropped

substantially. The $10,000 put away by a 40-year-old may grow to about $80,000 by age 58, which is a tidy little sum. But it sure won't provide much of an income from an SWP, and the thought that, if you had *only* chosen to invest in your 20s, you could have ended up with $640,000, is enough to make many a grown man or woman weep.

The difference, as you can see, is dramatic. As each decade of life passes, you need to save that much more, if you hope to have a comfortable retirement. If you are experiencing cash-flow problems in your 40s, you should definitely be considering leverage — especially if you have the security of a job, and have paid some money down on your house.

Leverage is a strategy in which you borrow to invest outside an RRSP. Interest payments on the loan for investment purposes are tax deductible. Therefore, interest-only payments on a loan are treated in a similar fashion as an RRSP deduction. They are both tax deductible. If you are in your 40s and have an extra free dollar, what should you do with it? First of all, maximize your RRSPs, without question, because of that "refund" from the government in the form of tax write-offs. However, if you have a good salary and a decent government pension, you may not have a large allowable RRSP limit to work with.

After maximizing your RRSP, you should try to eliminate all non-tax-deductible debt. But the longer it takes you to do this, the fewer compounding years you have left. What should you do?

Everyone in their 40s should have a financial plan done. The critical question here is, how much do you have to invest each year both inside and outside your RRSP to retire when you want with the income you want? Answering this question is the only way you will know what course of action is best for your particular situation.

The advantage of leveraging at this age is that you are creating an additional tax deduction that provides you with a tax rebate that can be used to pay down non-tax-deductible debt, while still permitting you to put money away for the future. You also have a larger amount of money working for you. (Read Chapter Eight for more details on this strategy.)

A lot of people dream of the day when they will finally be out of debt. Remember those compounding years and don't feel that being "in debt" is necessarily bad — it's the *kind* of debt you take on that is critical, and you must use that borrowed money wisely! These are the years when a financial plan is essential.

THE FINANCIALLY FURIOUS 50S

As you move into your 50s, there's a good chance that your children are approaching or are in their college or university years. You will soon be aware of just how costly post-secondary education is. This is when you really start shelling out money! If your children decide to go to a college in the United States, or in a Canadian city where you do not reside, the cost is even greater.

Although you are by now at the peak of your earning years, your expenses may also be at greater heights than in the past. A financial plan is still important for you because, once you edge into your 60s, you will not have as many years to see compounding work its magic before retirement. But, if you have just turned 50, you do still have fifteen years in which your money can double twice, and then even earn a little more.

In your 50s, it becomes critical to look at time — and you have very little of it to work with before retirement. This is when you want to be looking at embarking upon leverage-type programs, if you haven't already. If you have been successful in saving money outside of your RRSP, you should consider setting up a savings program inside a Universal Life Insurance program, to get tax-deferred growth on your money.

In their late 40s and early 50s people tend to be more willing to be aggressive with their investments. To be blunt, they hear the clock ticking. Alas, this is when many of them make large investments, such as borrowing to invest in an oil well, or making a risky move into limited partnerships. They are going for the "big hit," because they are beginning to realize they are going to retire in the not-too-distant future, and they "must do something!"

This is a problem. Because at this time of life you cannot afford to take major losses in risky ventures; you don't have the time for compounding to "make up" for any mistakes. This part bears repetition: In this period people must be more careful. I may appear to be making this statement in every decade, but don't forget: You can *afford* to take a loss or two in your 20s — look at the compounding time you have left ahead of you! But in your 50s, you just don't.

And remember as well that if companies are in a down-sizing mode (as I wrote these words, Boeing let go *tens of thousands* of employees around the world), the 50s are an awful decade to find yourself looking for a new position. Most 50-year-olds tend to be near the peak of their earning period and can always be replaced by a person in their early 30s at half the cost.

There are further problems with being in your 50s and out of work. You may not be as technologically competent or savvy or up-to-date as someone just coming out of trade school, college, or university in the 1990s. True, the latter do not possess your experience, but they were probably educated in the cutting-edge technology.

Most companies today have the same dilemma that a hockey team owner does: Should he hire a veteran and go for experience, knowing that the player may have only a few years left in him, and hope that he helps the bench? Or should he go with younger players, because they are the future? (And are much, much cheaper.)

Most people in their 50s feel as if they are in their prime of life, that they have never been more important and potent. And they often are. But in terms of society and employment (if not in health), they are, sadly, on a slippery slope.

THE SAGACIOUS 60S

By the time you reach your 60s, your die has essentially been cast. Unless you are expecting to inherit a lot of money, there is not much you can do at this point in your life to increase your wealth. You lack the compounding years, and what you're doing at this age is "completing the plan" and spending some of your money rather than accumulating it.

However, if you have invested predominantly in guaranteed financial vehicles, it is still not too late to shift into equities. Usually, though, at this point in life, most people *cannot* make a significant change in what their retirement is going to look like. (Unless, of course, they work until they are 70 or beyond, are making large sums of money, or have sold the family home, and are pocketing hundreds of thousands that they don't need to spend on shelter.)

In your 60s, it is very important to manage the money you have as effectively as possible. Taxes are a major consideration. Look at diversifying some non-RRSP funds into capital-gain and dividend-yielding investments. Make sure your portfolio is growing after taxes, inflation, and withdrawals. Two strategies that are excellent for 60+ investors are Systematic Withdrawal Plans (Chapter Ten) and Back-to-Backs, discussed in Chapter Fourteen.

Remember, you do need some growth from your investments. A general rule of thumb is to take your age and subtract it from one hundred. That is the smallest percentage of your investments you should put into good quality stocks or equity-based mutual funds.

There is an excellent chance that you will live to 80 or 90, so do not underestimate the amount of time your money will need to last. People are living longer than ever before. When you talk with seniors, the one thing you hear again and again is something like, "I've got this young mind that seems to be trapped in an aging, even old body! Where did all the time go?" Remember George Bernard Shaw's great aphorism that youth is wasted on the young? Indeed it is. One of the real problems with life in general (and financial planning in particular) is that you can't place an old and wise head on young shoulders. Wisdom is something that takes time. But to retire successfully, you do need to exercise wisdom at a younger age.

Message to All of You, in Any Decade of Your Life: Pay Yourself First!

The only way to save is to pay yourself first. Entire books have been written on this subject, and with good reason: It is critical to follow this advice. There is an old saying that "if you don't respect yourself, nobody else will." And this is never more true than when applied to putting aside money — in other words, you're worth paying!

What each of you must do is budget to set aside $100 or $200 every month, from the earliest age possible. You must look at this as "making a payment to yourself." This money should be part of your budget just like paying your rent or mortgage, cable bill, phone bill, and so on. Don't depend on extra money you might suddenly receive (a gift from granny, a Christmas bonus, a hundred-dollar pay-off from the provincial lottery).

You may find it hard to save. But you can change that. The first thing you have to do every month is to put yourself first in line as you apportion your pay. If you save, then invest, small amounts of money in your youth, you will have a significant amount of money in the future — at a time when you might truly need it: when your regular income has stopped.

If you don't start now, you will have to save proportionally far higher amounts at later stages in life. It is true that as you get older, your living costs should be reduced; however, your years in which to compound decrease. It is always difficult to save; if you want to see how very difficult it can be, talk to someone who is in their early 60s. (Especially those who failed to put away money in their 20s or 30s.)

One of the saddest and most frequent laments I hear from my clients is this: "Oh, Brent! I wish that somebody had told me about the importance of saving years ago! How I *wish* someone had told me!"

The previous generations had an excuse that we do not have at the end of the twentieth century, and the opening years of the twenty-first. Just two decades ago, discussing finances was even more taboo than sex. Nobody talked about money; it was hard to get information. Business pages in newspapers were few and far between.

Today, information about investing, stocks, bonds, mutual funds, etc., is everywhere, from the radio to the TV to the Internet to the daily newspapers. There is no excuse for not knowing about finances today — and you must do something about managing your own!

THE POWER OF COMPOUNDING

When I speak with young clients, one of the things I hear the most is, "I just don't have enough money to invest! I have to save up some cash, first."

This is simply not true. As a matter of fact, many mutual funds permit you to invest as little as $25 a month. They will withdraw the amount you specify out of your bank account automatically. It is just like a loan payment, and it compounds, so it is not like some of the life insurance programs, or like banks, which insist that you must accumulate $500 before you can buy a GIC.

Take a look at the first chart in Appendix Two. This table, which shows the value of $100, invested over forty years, demonstrates the extraordinary power of compounding. The second chart in this appendix shows the potential growth of your investment if you deposit $100 every month for twenty-five years. Watch how your investment grows. And grows.

UNDERSTAND AND BECOME
COMFORTABLE WITH VOLATILITY

I suggest that people start their investing by putting their money into equities. For the long term — and that's what we're discussing here — always invest in equities. This is the only area where you are truly going to encounter the miracle and joy of compounding. Although it can often feel painful when the market "goes through a correction," you should remain happy and continue to invest, because you are buying shares "on sale" at that time.

A classic example is the Tale of the Tuna Fish. You go to the supermarket and you purchase tuna fish. Normally, it's $2.29, but one day when you are shopping for various other items, you discover an amazing sale — only $0.99 a tin for your favourite brand of tuna fish!

Oh, you like this. You like this a lot. What do you do? Do you fill your basket with ten, twenty, even thirty cans, to take advantage of this wonderful deal? Or do you go right home, thinking, "The price of tuna fish is going to drop to zero! I should sell off all the expensive cans I already have at home!"

When people hear me describe this classic example, they think that second response is an absurd reaction. I would like to submit, however, that this is *exactly* what most people do when they are investing!

Think about it. When investments (stocks, bonds, or mutual funds) drop in value, the first thing most people want to do is sell them! "Oh, heavens!" they say to themselves (possibly using a more vulgar expression), "If my investments keep decreasing in value, I'll have no money left!" Of course, the proper, thoughtful thing to do — like the wise shopper who loads up on cans of that suddenly much cheaper tuna fish — is to buy more when prices have fallen. (Naturally, if it's a sale on milk, yogurt, cheese, or something else that is time dated and can "go bad," this analogy doesn't work. Which is why I use tuna fish in my example.)

This strange, self-destructive, almost absurd response to falling prices leads me to ask a painful question: Do you know where your money is invested?

"In mutual funds," you may well answer.

Sure, it's in mutual funds. But *what stocks* are in each of those funds? When you receive your regular reports, do you look to see what your funds have been buying for their portfolios? Do you recognize any of these companies? Do you know what they do? (If you are vehemently opposed to smoking or liquor consumption, you'd better make sure that your various funds aren't investing your money in companies who manufacture and/or sell these products.)

These are questions that all of you, as wise investors, must ask yourselves: What does each company do? What do they make? Do I, as a consumer, actually purchase, use, or support this product?

If you don't ask these questions, you really *don't* know where your money is. And that's a pretty good reason to feel concerned and even frightened when a mutual fund drops in price.

However, if you bought shares of the Royal Bank or CIBC or Coca-Cola or Walt Disney or Gillette or Nike or Bombardier — or mutual funds that buy shares in those great firms — would you be scared when their prices dropped a bit? Would you be fearful that any one of those might go bankrupt? Do you honestly believe that the day will come when any of them will no longer exist, like a typewriter firm or a company that makes buggy whips?

You have very little to worry about when you're dealing in shares in international conglomerates (or at least international success stories) such as these. You should feel reasonably assured that they will be around, that they will rebound in price after a correction, and likely sooner rather than later. (In the case of Royal Bank and CIBC, if you *really* feared for their future, you wouldn't have allowed your employer to deposit your paycheques in one of their banks every week or every month over the years!)

When this very emotional situation arises — when stock prices fall — and you have a passionate, obsessive desire to sell, slow down and ask yourself, "Should I truly be worried about losing my money with this investment?" If you don't have any idea of what companies you have been investing in, either by yourself or through your mutual fund company, then no wonder you panic!

If you are the panicking type — and who is not, occasionally? — it's only logical that you should ensure that a significant portion of your investments are in solid, blue-chip stocks that you really don't have to worry about. I have great faith in a mutual fund company like Infinity (but I am a partial owner of that firm, so I have a vested interest).

But, even if I had no connection with that rapidly growing family of funds, it would still fit into my thesis here. I'm willing to bet that 99% of all investors would recognize the names and products of 80% of Infinity's investments, if not more. And even if you have no involvement with the stock market, you probably use a lot of the products produced by the companies in Infinity's portfolio. Once you understand a company and are comfortable with it, you are more likely to react like the thoughtful Tuna Fish Shopper: You will want to stock up when its price is low, and not run and sell all you have the moment its price dips.

We are all in an instant-gratification culture now. We have

used that philosophy to guide our lives and, much worse, to guide our investments. Wise investors don't worry about fluctuations in prices, and are usually very successful in their financial stability. They think about investments over the long term. These investments can be regarded almost like young children. They are growing; there may be periods when they don't shoot up, or their growth is infinitesimal, but they will continue to grow. And the investors realize that slow growth is the way they will accumulate wealth. They don't always look only at their own wealth and savings, they look at the future generations' wealth, too.

REGARDLESS OF YOUR DECADE, DON'T SPREAD OUT TOO THIN!

To further this issue of "knowing where you are putting your money," another thought arises: If you purchase sixty, eighty, even a hundred different stocks, it would be impossible to know all of those companies. True, banks are doing well, but what about oil? And can gold be trusted to be strong next year? You could never follow the "fortunes" of all of them. Yet if you purchase a dozen or two dozen mutual funds, you make keeping track of them impossible! After all, each mutual fund has between fifty and two hundred major stocks in its portfolio at any one time.

Most experts feel that the optimum number of mutual funds that anyone needs to own is seven. Any more than that is simply not necessary. Yet I have seen people with $1 million — even $100,000 — who put their money in thirty or more mutual funds! If you examined the stocks in those mutual funds, you'd probably find a great deal of duplication.

Somehow, people must turn their thinking around to the "Tuna Fish" way. When you see the price of your investments drop in value, you must see a glorious opportunity to buy more. Imagine if I were to suddenly hand you a 25%-off coupon on your next grocery bill — or a 25%-off coupon on the purchase of your next car. Would you hesitate for a single nanosecond?

Yet most people treat the "25%-off coupon" (which is offered now and then, thanks to market corrections) in a different way when it comes to stocks and mutual funds. Tuna fish is one thing, most people feel, and investments are another.

This incorrect thinking occurs because people allow their emotions to take over when they are dealing with their assets, their future, and their retirement. "Where's the door? I'm *outta* here!" is what too many say when the market becomes volatile or drops (seemingly) precipitously. Yet if a consumer product drops in price, whether tuna fish or a VCR, most will run out and buy it.

Invest in products that you know, respect, and use. Look at downturns in the stock market as opportunities to invest. If you wish to get ahead and have more money to spend and enjoy in the years to come, you have to do what others are *not* doing. And what most others are doing is panicking and dumping their stocks, instead of buying, when the price drops.

If you understand that quality companies compound in value over time, whether it be great international conglomerates or Canadian banks — companies you feel comfortable with — how could you not borrow to invest in such great firms?

That is why I called this book *Tortoise Wins the Race.* The tortoise, who invests wisely, thoughtfully, knowledgeably, and as early (and often) as possible, will beat the speedy (and risk-taking) hare — every single time.

CHAPTER SEVEN

Investing the Warren Buffett Way

M ost investors have heard the statistics that show that 80%
of the mutual funds available for purchase today have
not managed to outperform their respective indexes. Despite
this fact, the number of mutual funds being marketed to
the public continues to grow. When you're researching mutual
funds, the best question you can ask yourself is "How can I
make sure that the mutual fund I purchase performs well?"

To answer this question, it is best to look to the teachings
of the most successful investor in North America, probably in
the world: Warren Buffett (and his mentor, Benjamin Graham).
His investment strategy is so logical and basic, it is almost
absurd that most investors do not follow it. I will highlight the
key principles of his philosophy.

Buffett believes that an investor should invest only in large
companies that have shareholder-oriented management and a
dominant position in their market, with consistent growth and
profit. Once he finds these companies, his "favorite holding
period is forever." He feels that diversification is over-rated, and
investors should instead be concentrating on companies that
meet the criteria set out above. If they don't, they will reduce
their gains by over-diversifying. Buffett also believes that it is
time *in* the market that counts, not the timing *of* the market.

This boring, lacklustre, unexciting, time-and-tax-efficient strategy has managed to average a compounded, per annum return over the last five, ten, and fifteen years of "only" 31%, 30%, and 30%, respectively. (Try to achieve that in a GIC or Canada Savings Bond — or in any mutual fund around the world, for that matter!) These numbers represent the return of Warren Buffett's investment company, Berkshire Hathaway Inc. Class A, as of December 31, 1998.

If we employ the rule of 72 to see how long it would take your money to double at a 30% per annum compounded return, we find that it would take 2.4 years. (The rule of 72 helps us to determine how long it takes money to double. You divide 72 by the annual percentage growth to determine the number of years needed for this happy occurrence to take place. If there is 3% growth in your investment per year, divide 72 by 3 to discover that the money will double in twenty-four years; 6% annual growth means that it will take twelve years for the amount to double; 9% annual growth means it will take eight years for a doubling of the investment, and so on.) Past performance is no guarantee of future performance, as mutual fund prospectuses are always informing us. How has your portfolio performed? Maybe a strategy change is in order!

To my knowledge, there are only two mutual fund companies in Canada that adhere to Buffett's principles. They are the Infinity Group of Funds and the AIC Group of Funds (which are competitors in the marketplace). As I own a very tiny percentage of Infinity stock, I will refer to that company; however, with regard to their underlying principles — "the Warren Buffett Way" of investing — both fund families are similar. In my opinion, every investor in Canada should own at least one of the funds offered by these two excellent companies.

Nearly all non-Buffett-style equity portfolio managers purchase stocks when they are undervalued, with a view to selling them when the price has gone up. Generally speaking, the average holding period is five years: Portfolio managers will buy and sell all of your investments in the fund every five years. Every time you sell a stock, you trigger a capital gain or loss, depending on whether the value of the stock went up or down. This leads to an important question: Have you ever stopped to consider the tax efficiency of your investment?

The chart on the next page compares periodic trading to the buy-and-hold strategy. To simplify the example, I have assumed that all the growth in the buy-and-hold strategy is capital gains and that no dividends are triggered by the investments. (This of course is not what usually happens.) For the periodic trading, I have assumed that the full growth capital gains are triggered every five years. (This also is not completely accurate, as dividends would be triggered every year and usually some of the stocks are sold every year.)

The use of both of these assumptions equalizes the two examples, making the comparison fair. Each column assumes a return of 10%, a capital gains tax rate of 35%, with only capital gains being earned, and equal investments of $200,000.

After thirty years, the $200,000 in the periodic trading column would have grown to $735,556, or a 4.4% compounded per annum return after tax. The buy-and-hold strategy would have grown to $2,338,422 after tax, for an 8.5% compounded per annum return. Doesn't this represent a huge difference?

Of course it does! Who would not love to have an additional $1.5 million to enjoy at retirement? And the key advantage is simply the tax deferral!

Do *you* believe in the buy-and-hold strategy for your mutual funds? It doesn't matter if you don't trade your funds; if your portfolio manager does the trading — and almost all of them do — you are simply not achieving your desired results! You should invest in mutual funds like Infinity, where the money manager follows the buy-and-hold strategy, if you want to maximize the tax deferral.

Generally, when we purchase a mutual fund, we look at the track record and then make sure that the current portfolio

PERIODIC TRADING VERSUS BUY AND HOLD

		Amount invested			$200,000	
		Rate of return			10.0%	
		Marginal tax rate — capital gains			35.0%	

| | Periodic trading | | | Buy and hold | | |
End of year	Growth	Tax payable	After-tax value	Growth	Tax payable	After-tax value
1	20,000	–	220,000	20,000	–	220,000
2	22,000	–	242,000	22,000	–	242,000
3	24,200	–	266,200	24,200	–	266,200
4	26,620	–	292,820	26,620	–	292,820
5	29,282	42,736	279,366	29,282	–	322,102
6	27,937	–	307,303	32,210	–	354,312
7	30,730	–	338,033	35,431	–	389,743
8	33,803	–	371,837	38,974	–	428,718
9	37,184	–	409,020	42,872	–	471,590
10	40,902	87,473	362,449	47,159	–	518,748
11	36,245	–	398,694	51,875	–	570,623
12	39,869	–	438,564	57,062	–	627,686
13	43,856	–	482,420	62,769	–	690,454
14	48,242	–	530,662	69,045	–	759,500
15	53,066	134,305	449,423	75,950	–	835,450
16	44,945	–	494,366	83,545	–	918,995
17	49,437	–	543,802	91,899	–	1,010,894
18	54,380	–	598,183	101,089	–	1,111,983
19	59,818	–	658,001	111,198	–	1,223,182
20	65,800	183,330	540,471	122,318	–	1,345,500
21	54,047	–	594,518	134,550	–	1,480,050
22	59,452	–	653,970	148,005	–	1,628,055
23	65,397	–	719,366	162,805	–	1,790,860
24	71,937	–	791,303	179,086	–	1,969,947
25	79,130	234,652	635,782	196,995	–	2,166,941
26	63,578	–	699,360	216,694	–	2,383,635
27	69,936	–	769,296	238,364	–	2,621,999
28	76,930	–	846,225	262,200	–	2,884,199
29	84,623	–	930,848	288,420	–	3,172,619
30	93,085	288,376	735,556	317,262	1,151,458	2,338,422
After-Tax Return			4.4%			8.5%

manager actually earned that return. After looking at the volatility, we decide whether to purchase it. Hence, many people are reluctant to purchase funds with short track records. (And Infinity came into existence only in early 1997.)

One of the advantages of investing in a fund that follows the Warren Buffett philosophy is that a fund does not need a long track record. It is the track records of the individual stocks, and their future prospects, that matter!

In Appendix Three, you will find the portfolios of the Infinity International, Canadian, and Wealth Management funds, along with the five-, ten-, and fifteen-year performance of the stocks in their portfolio, as of December 31, 1998.

Take a moment and look down the list of these companies. How many of them do you recognize? If you owned, say, the Infinity International Fund, and the market dropped 20%, would you be afraid that you would lose all of your money? Of course not. Look at the names of these firms — they are all market leaders. Now, take a look at the portfolios of the mutual funds you presently own. How many of their companies do you recognize? How many of their products do you have in your home, have you drunk, worn, used, or invested in recently?

I hope I have made my point.

Infinity has published an excellent pamphlet, called *Infinity Owner's Manual*, which is sent to all first-time investors in their fund family. It outlines their investment philosophy and answers many of the most frequently asked questions. With their permission, I am reprinting two of their pages below. I have probably read these words hundreds of times. If you read them even once, it could have a profound effect upon your retirement years and even on the future security of your children.

What should you do if the stock market goes down?
Nothing, ignore it. The stock market is irrelevant. Much like a spectator at a baseball game who keeps his eye on the playing field and occasionally glances at the scoreboard, keep your

eyes on the fundamentals of Infinity's businesses. Has anything changed? The scoreboard is the stock market and from time to time it might malfunction.

It was Warren Buffett's mentor, Benjamin Graham, who taught him how to think about the stock market:

"The stock market is a manic-depressive fellow who comes to work everyday, offering to buy something from you or sell something to you. The more depressed Mr. Market is, the wider his swings in his offering prices," i.e. during the 1990 Gulf War, Mr. Market became very depressed and scared, and offered to sell shares of Berkshire Hathaway at U.S. $5,600. Today these shares are worth U.S. $59,000 (October 1998).

Mr. Market should either be ignored or exploited depending on your financial situation. This manic-depressive fellow, therefore, should never be your guide, but simply your servant.

What should you do about the influences exerted by the market, politics, economic forecasters and newspapers?
Ignore them. To quote from the 1994 Berkshire Hathaway Annual Report:

We will continue to ignore political and economic forecasts, which are an expensive distraction for many investors and businessmen. Thirty years ago, no one could have foreseen the huge expansion of the Vietnam War, wage and price controls, two oil shocks, the resignation of a President, the dissolution of the Soviet Union, a one-day drop in the Dow of 508 points, or Treasury Bill yields fluctuating between 2.8% and 17.4%.

But surprise — none of these blockbuster events made the slightest dent in Ben Graham's investment principles. Nor did they render unsound the negotiated purchases of fine businesses at sensible prices. Imagine the cost to us, then, if we had let the fear of unknowns cause us to defer or alter the deployment of capital. Indeed we have usually made our purchases when apprehensions about some macro event were at a peak. Fear is the foe of the faddist, but the friend of the fundamentalist.

A different set of major shocks is sure to occur in the next thirty years. We will neither try to predict them nor profit from them. If we can identify businesses similar to those we have purchased in the past, external surprises will have little effect on our long-term results.

If this chapter has sparked your interest, I strongly recommend the following books:

- *The Warren Buffett Way*, by Robert G. Hagstrom Jr., published by John Wiley and Sons, Inc. This book was given to me by Richard Charlton, an investment advisor in Toronto, who is probably one of the most successful advisors in Canada, measured by how much money he has made for his clients. He is a devout Warren Buffett follower, as can be seen by the next recommendation:
- *Invest the Billionaire's Way: The Genius of Patience* by Richard Charlton (one of the founders of the Infinity Group of Funds).
- Finally, if you are the type of Canadian who made *Coles Notes* and *Reader's Digest* so popular, the *Infinity Owner's Manual* is perfect for you — it's short and to the point, and an excellent read.

Remember that past performance is no guarantee of future performance, and mutual funds are sold by prospectus only. Ask your financial advisor for one, and take a look at the above books when you're next in the library or bookstore.

Chapter Eight

Borrowing To Invest (a.k.a. Leveraging)

A number of fine books have been written on the subject of borrowing to invest. A good one, *The Strategy*, was written by former Member of Parliament and present TV-business broadcaster Garth Turner. Well-known speakers on financial matters, such as Brian Costello and Jerry White, also talk about this kind of financial manoeuvre.

"Leveraging" and "borrowing to invest" are different names used to describe the same strategy. If you borrow to invest money outside the RRSP, the interest-only payments on the loan are tax deductible. (Interest payments on RRSP loans are not tax deductible.) If you decide to make principal payments on the loan, these payments are not tax deductible.

Most people feel that the main reason for borrowing money to invest is to get more money working for them and thus increase their profit potential. For example, let's assume that you have borrowed $100,000. And let's say that this loan is costing you 8% annually (investment loans are usually prime or prime-plus-one). Your interest cost over a twelve-month period would be $8,000 on that $100,000 loan. You can choose to make interest-only payments on the loan (making your full payment tax deductible), or interest plus principal. The principal payments would not be tax deductible.

If you are in the 50% marginal tax bracket — to make the numbers clean and easy here — you will receive a $4,000 refund from Revenue Canada for taking out this $100,000 loan! (Interesting, isn't it, that this refund of four grand would be exactly the same as if you had put $8,000 into your RRSP.)

This $8,000 interest expense would go into your income tax under the line "interest and carrying charges." As its effect works its way through your return, the result is that the net cost of that loan is about $4,000 a year. To put it another way: The cost of borrowing $100,000 will be a mere 4%. Not bad, eh?

Let's make a fair assumption: With your $100,000 loan, you are able to invest in financial vehicles that will achieve a 10% annual return. So you make $10,000 a year, while shelling out some $4,000 for that loan. In other words, you have turned $4,000 into $10,000, which is a 250% return. Also, not too bad!

Many people will look at what I've just written (or told them) and declare, "Brent, I was raised by parents who echoed Polonius in Shakespeare's *Hamlet*, when he declared, "Neither a borrower nor a lender be." Why on earth should I take out such a large loan — and why would I want to maintain this loan year after year? When would I pay it off?" The idea is that you do not pay it off — and this often causes some apprehension at first, in the neither-a-borrower-nor-a-lender-be generation.

We have seen how interest costs on a loan for investment purposes are treated but what about principal payments?

If you wanted to pay down the principal by $5,000, what would your before-tax cost be if you were at the 50% marginal tax bracket? You would have to earn $10,000 and pay Revenue Canada $5,000 to pay the loan down by $5,000.

If you have the cash flow to pay down the principal, that's fine, but it is more tax efficient to pay interest-only costs. In the future, you can cash out some of the gains to pay down the loan principal, if you desire.

WHY TAKE UNNECESSARY RISKS?

When I sit down with clients to discuss their risk tolerance, they will often declare, "I am medium risk" or "I am high risk." In the latter case, they usually wish to invest their money — borrowed or not — into sector-specific markets that tend to be a little more volatile than most: for example, Asia, Latin America, emerging markets, or resources.

As we all know — especially after the difficult, roller-coaster summer of 1998 — those areas have been volatile in a not-particularly-desirable way, and they have lost money over the past few years. However, at other times, those sectors have been known to grow by as much as 60% a year. Which leads to a question I pose to my clients, and pose to you here:

Why would you choose to invest in those areas? What real gains are achieved in such volatile situations?

My clients' answer is, invariably, that their goal is "to make more money!" But you must look at the risk, as well as the reward, in everything. A 50% return on an investment (stock, mutual fund, whatever) in a year is marvellous. But when that 50% goes in the *opposite* direction, can you handle it?

To really invest properly and wisely in any of those sectors, you must either hold for the long term and ride all the manic-depressive fluctuations, or try to time the market. And, as I've noted elsewhere in this book, nobody has been able to time the market — jump in and out at the best possible moments — consistently over a long period of time. It's simply not possible.

Hence, this strategy is flawed to begin with. Which leads to the following suggestion, which I always make to my clients. (Note that what I'm going to suggest may be contrary to what many others recommend, but we're here to explore new ideas, aren't we?) Here goes:

Even if you are the most aggressive, risk-taking investor, why would you invest in aggressive investments at all? Why take such risks, when I can give you financial vehicles with a very low volatility rate (let's say two, on a scale of one to ten, as ranked by the *National Post*, with ten being the highest risk), investments that have averaged 10% to 15% per year returns over a ten-year period?

If you have borrowed to buy into these investments — let's go back to our $100,000 loan of before — you would have made a 250% return before tax if you had cashed that investment in! (And that's with earning only 10%, not 15%, on your $100,000 loan, while paying $8,000 interest and writing off $4,000 of that on your income tax return.)

What are the chances that, if you invest in a highly volatile or speculative stock (or sector of the market), you will average a 250% return in a single year? I would suggest it's very slim.

Let's look at something like the Templeton Growth Fund, one of the truly great mutual funds of the past four decades. It has averaged a little over 15% a year throughout that lengthy period of time. Though I'm not about to suggest that such remarkable gains will continue forever, if Templeton Growth continued to average that 15% compounded per annum return, the $4,000 carrying cost of your $100,000 loan would be overwhelmed by some $15,000 a year — which is nearly a 400% return on your money — slightly more than the 1% or 2% you receive in your savings account at your friendly neighbourhood bank, or the 5% (or less) you can land with a GIC!

What's the risk? Your only risk is the one that is taken for the underlying investment. My question is, are you comfortable with a non-fly-by-night company like Templeton Growth? How about Fidelity International Portfolio?

All of these types of investments have had excellent track records. Look at Infinity International. It follows the Warren Buffett School of long-term, quality-company investing: Coca-Cola, Walt Disney, Gillette, Bombardier, bank stocks. Can you imagine (in your wildest nightmares) that you might someday wake up to discover that any of those conglomerates, international corporations, and financial institutions would not be in existence? We're not discussing a recently-turned-capitalistic Russia here; these companies are some of the most impressive, rock-solid companies on the face of the planet, and some of the greatest business success stories in history.

Of course, they will be around! Sure, they'll all go through periods of volatility, and their prices may well jump up and down, 5%, 10%, or even more. You don't have to look further back than the summer of 1998 to prove this fact. Yet I love to remind people of the Great Crash of October 1987, when everyone thought that the world had come to an end, that the Golden Goose had finally been cooked. Stocks on the New York and Toronto Stock Exchanges took a dive, and people envisioned brokers leaping off the eightieth stories of their financial houses. Yet when December 31, 1987, rolled around, it was noted — though by very few, in fact — that the TSE and Dow Jones Averages of that entire year were still up nearly 5%, over the entire, scary, volatile twelve-month period! So much for the end of the world.

I like to ask home owners to think of their own home for a moment. House prices also go through volatile periods, and one should expect that. Would you ever consider purchasing some real estate, only to sell within a year of buying it? Most would consider that speculation. But because anything can happen in the short term and you'd have to pay those 7% (or so) real estate fees, your actions would be quite aggressive and risky.

Of course, most people — at least 95% — see the purchase of a home as a very long-term proposition. They often intend to keep it for ten, even twenty years. They don't view this as aggressive investing at all, do they?

Risk is usually related to how long you plan to hold on to something, whether it be Gillette stock or a two-bedroom bungalow. Why wouldn't you transpose the knowledge and life experience learned from buying a home to other investments, which work much the same way?

The difference between real estate and, say, a mutual fund

is that over a long period of time, the Standard and Poor Index may average around 13% per year in growth, whereas the Real Estate Index has averaged around 4% to 5%. The latter more or less keeps up with inflation.

When you invest in a quality, proven-by-time-and-record vehicle such as a quality stock or mutual fund, you're dealing with a solid asset that has outperformed real estate by two to three times, on an annual basis! The trick is — and it's not a very sneaky trick — to keep your portfolio in conservative international funds, or bank stocks, or whatever type of investment you are comfortable with that you know will be around in the long term, and simply borrow to invest.

WHAT ARE SOME OF THE BENEFITS OF THIS STRATEGY?

By borrowing to invest, you are creating a legal, acceptable, generous tax deduction. If you feel we pay far too much tax in Canada, you are not alone in that belief. Most of us feel that way. Our marginal tax rates are far too high; compared with the top marginal tax rate in the United States (less than 40%), our tax burden is exceedingly onerous.

What deductions can you receive from fairly low-risk investments over the long term? There aren't many left. The federal government gives tax advantages to certain industries, such as the oil industry, where they try to encourage companies to drill for oil. These firms then flow the tax deduction through to the investor. The investor thus gets a tax deduction for making the investment — hence the name flow-through shares. Flow-through shares and limited partnerships offer large deductions. However, you have a strong chance of losing some or all of your money. I would recommend caution before embarking on such investments.

Let me give you another example. Let's say that you are a typical Canadian family, with a home, a mortgage, and 2.1 kids. You're young — probably in your 30s. As I noted earlier, the cost of raising a family is ferociously expensive in this country and in this day and age, especially if only one spouse is working. (You don't have to be a card-carrying feminist to recognize that women who stay at home and raise their children are certainly working — often a lot harder than their office-attending husbands — but the financial remuneration tends to be a lot less generous.)

It is hard to live well on a single income at the turn of the millennium, even if the one money-producing spouse is making $40 to $50 thousand a year. Usually these families try to maximize their RRSP, because they want that tax deduction. Other than that, they are not able to do very much saving and investing.

Let's look at this situation more closely. Assume you are managing to save $1,000 a year. In order to save $1,000 of after-tax income, you will have to earn some $2,000, since you probably have to pay close to $1,000 of that to Revenue Canada for the privilege of being Canadian. You buy groceries, diapers, etc., and you stagger on financially, from month to month, year to year.

What if you were able to take the $2,000 a year gross income (before tax) and use it to pay the interest cost on a loan for investment purposes? If your interest-only cost was 8%, you would be able to borrow $25,000 to invest. (I will explain how to do this later in this chapter.) The form you use to accomplish this is called a "tax deductions at source form," a copy of which is found in Appendix Four. By submitting this form, you are telling Revenue Canada that rather than waiting for the end of the year to get a refund for the interest deduction or RRSP deduction, you want your refund paid monthly. This will solve your cash flow problem.

You take that $2,000, out of which you normally have to send $1,000 to Revenue Canada in taxes, and use it to pay the interest on that $25,000 loan. Remember, that $2,000 interest you're paying is tax deductible, so, as before, Revenue Canada is "paying you back" some $1,000 instead of you paying them!

If that $25,000 you have borrowed to invest gives you a 10% return per annum, you have now earned $2,500 over twelve months. Although your investment is $25,000, it is not your money; it is the bank's and you will have to pay it back. Your true out-of-pocket cost is the $1,000 interest that you spent. Hence, your $1,000 investment would have grown to $2,500 (if sold), 2.5 times your money, in one year.

I have included two charts in Appendix Five that show you the difference between saving $1,000 a year and borrowing $25,000 to invest. Your net out-of-pocket expense, assuming a 50% marginal tax bracket, is exactly the same: $1,000 a year. A 10% return is assumed, and both investments are assumed to grow completely tax free. (This is, of course, not realistic as there would be some distribution triggered by the fund each year. However, we have no way to guess how much the distribution would be.)

After twenty-five years, the $1,000 a year investment grew to $98,347, while the $25,000 loan grew to $270,868, minus the $25,000 loan, $245,868. This is a difference of $147,521!

Remember, these figures are before-tax examples, so to make it more realistic, let's assume both investments are completely sold at the end of twenty-five years. It's important that you be able to calculate this for yourself, so I have included the calculation for you to follow:

$1,000-a-year investment		$25,000 leverage plan	
$98,347		$270,868	
− 25,000	dollars invested	− 25,000	repayment of loan
73,347	profit	245,868	
− 18,337	(25% tax-free capital gains)	− 61,467	25% tax free
55,010	taxable	184,401	taxable
− 27,505	50% tax payable	− 92,200	tax payable
$27,505		$92,200	

After-tax return	After-tax return
$27,505	$ 92,200
+ 18,337 (25% tax free)	+ 61,467 25% tax free
+ 25,000 invested money	
$70,842	$153,667

On an after-tax basis, the leverage program would net you $153,667 versus $70,842 from the $1,000-a-year program. That's an advantage of $82,825 for the same investment, same return, and same tax.

The difference between these two strategies is immense. If you are a normal Canadian, you are probably saying, "This all looks fine on paper, Brent. However, it doesn't work for me on a cash-flow basis! You see, I can only work with the net pay that my employer pays me after tax is withheld. Where do I get the cash flow to tide me over until I receive my refund over a year later?"

This is a most intuitive question, and asking it shows that you are truly grasping the concept. Bravo.

Refer to the form in Appendix Four, which should solve your problems and answer your excellent question. The Request for a Reduction of Tax Deductions at Source permits you to request that Revenue Canada instruct your employer's payroll department to pay you your income tax refunds (as per copies of paperwork included with form) as they are earned, rather than waiting until you file your tax return to get a refund. This means that your paycheque will increase each pay period, freeing up additional cash, which will allow you to invest more money! Let's look at an example:

Assume that you are entitled to contribute $4,000 to an RRSP after your pension adjustment is calculated. In consultation with your advisor, you have decided that you would like to take out a loan for investment purposes, to help you reach your retirement goals. So far, you have only been able to maximize your RRSP, but have not had the additional cash to do anything else. What do you do? (For the purpose of this example, we will assume that you are at the 50% marginal tax bracket.)

Currently, you are investing $4,000 into an RRSP; if you implement the "tax deductions at source" form, an additional $2,000 in cashflow will be freed up over the course of the calendar year. If you use the $2,000 to pay the tax-deductible interest costs on a loan, a further $1,000 will be freed up by submitting another form.

I think you get the idea. The net result is that if you are currently investing $4,000 each year in your RRSP, you can double your cash flow to $8,000 simply by using the refund to invest in another tax-deductible strategy; in other words, leveraging. Without adjusting your current situation, you would be able to afford a $50,000 loan, with interest-only payments at 8%, simply by using the Request for a Reduction of Tax Deductions at Source.

Clearly, you would not want to submit eight forms in a row to arrive at the desired result! This would not endear you to your payroll department, to say the least. Simply do the calculation above, using your top marginal tax bracket, and submit a single form. Remember, you are required to submit a form each year, so that Revenue Canada knows that you still have the tax deductions.

The numbers clearly show that, over the long term, borrowing to invest makes a great deal of sense. The Request for a Reduction of Tax Deductions at Source permits you to free up the cash to maximize your RRSP (if you were previously not able to do so), and/or take out a loan for investment purposes. Of course, nothing in life is free. There can be negatives. Let's look at a few.

SOME WORST-CASE SCENARIOS

What happens if there is a large market correction? If the market drops, say, 20%, you could potentially — if you had borrowed $50,000 to invest — lose $10,000. Of course, as the old saying goes, "you haven't lost money until you sell." But you must still be cautious. Depending on where you borrowed that money, you may receive what is known as "a margin call." This means that if the value of your investment drops below a certain "call" level, the bank will phone you up and ask you (politely, one hopes) to put more money in or to pay off the loan.

What such a call could do (at the worst possible time) is cement your loss. Before you borrow to invest, you must be aware of this very real possibility, and you must take certain precautions. Make sure that you can cover a margin call should it become necessary. At worst, you could be forced to sell your investment at its lowest point and worst price. So you must have some money sitting on the side somewhere to cover this, or you should have an asset to use as collateral, which would not be subject to a margin call. (Examples of this would be your home, GICs, or other assets). A home is going to keep its value, so there will be no problem if you want to use it as collateral for a secured line of credit. Many banks and trust companies have excellent loan programs, which your financial advisor should be aware of.

When you borrow to invest, you also have to be careful *where* you invest that money. Your goal should be investments that are low risk, as I discussed before. Avoid the temptation — and I've seen so many people fall for this! — to borrow to invest in Asia or Latin America. "If a 10% return on $50,000 will make me $5,000," many clients tell me, practically drooling with greedy, breathless anticipation, "imagine what a 40% return would make me! Why, I could make more money than I earn in a year!"

Sure. And you could also lose more money than you earn in a year. It's simply not worth the risk. Remember, financial planning does not happen overnight. If you want that kind of "financial planning," consider purchasing 6/49 tickets or Lucky

Lotto 7, or whatever "tax on the stupid" your province is offering. Good luck with your one-in-five-million chance of winning.

With my clients, I look for low-risk strategies to try to achieve decent growth on their investments. Because there is a further concern — and it is no small matter, in these times of downsizing, major mergers between giant companies, and other unexpected blows of fate. If you should lose your job, you'll still have the interest costs on that money you wisely borrowed to invest. What will you do then? To allow for even far-fetched possibilities, you must make sure not to borrow too much money.

The amount of money you borrow (to invest) must be within your limits, so that if you do lose your job, or suddenly have massive bills (whether a costly leak in your roof or a personal disability), you'll still be able to cope with the payments.

Another precaution you should take on behalf of a standard loan is to take life insurance out on it. Just term insurance, of course, an annual renewable term, in the same manner as you would insure your mortgage in case you or your spouse were to die. If the higher-income-earning spouse were to die, the loan would be paid off by the insurance company, and the surviving spouse would have the investment, free of the loan.

THEY CALL IT THE GOLDEN RULE FOR A REASON

You should always do everything in life within the bounds of reason. There should be a balance. Alas, one of the problems with money is that greed almost invariably rears its ugly head. And to me, one of the duties and responsibilities of a responsible financial advisor is to help regulate that ever-present greed so common to most of us.

Unfortunately, for a lot of people in my business, greed is one of the major motivators of our actions. "You should invest in Bre-X," many stockbrokers told their clients, "because it looks great! It'll make tons of money, and so will you!" Greed causes people to do things that they would not normally do with their money, as much as lust drives people into unfortunate, even dangerous sexual activities. Always make decisions based on logic — not on emotion.

Of course, this is far easier said than done.

My rule of thumb is: There is no such thing as a perfect investment, or a once-in-a-lifetime opportunity. I think long and hard about everything I am considering doing, and about what my clients want or hope to do. When money is involved, a bird in the hand . . .

You must be especially careful to understand everything you do. So if you plan to borrow to invest, I urge you to start off slowly.

For instance, be very aware of, and sensitive to, market conditions. If the stock market is incredibly high — as it was into the summer of 1998 — even if you love the borrowing-to-invest strategy, and even if it's for the long term, act differently and more conservatively than you normally do. Why not divide the amount you ultimately want to borrow over a twelve-month period?

What you would be doing, in effect, is "dollar cost averaging" while borrowing to invest. In other words, you are buying into that high market over a period of time. In this way, you would be averaging your purchase price.

True, if the market shoots up, you would probably brood a bit and murmur, "Boy, I wish I had invested everything at once! Look at all the gains I would have made!" But if the market suddenly dropped 20%, you'd be saying something quite different: "Thank goodness!"

SOME EXCITING NEW
STRATEGIES FOR YOU TO CONSIDER

The Manulife GIF

Manulife has recently come up with a relatively new strategy. It is called the Manulife GIF, or Guaranteed Investment Fund. The GIF is a very interesting investment, and if you're looking at borrowing to invest, it has some positive aspects you should be aware of.

Recall some of those negatives about borrowing to invest. The first negative was the margin call — the bank could require you, almost overnight, to put more money up to cover your "bet" (which is why I told you to invest and not bet, to choose financial vehicles carefully, and not to "play" the market). The second risk is that there is no floor under your investment. Technically speaking, your investment could always drop down to zero (which is why I suggest conservative, time-proven, truly great companies, such as national banks, Walt Disney, Coca-Cola, and so on, or mutual funds that hold such quality stocks).

Here's how the Manulife GIF loan program works. When you put in $25,000 of non-RRSP money, Manulife will give you a loan of up to four-to-one. In other words, they will loan you up to $100,000, using that $25,000 and the borrowed investment as collateral. They will advance it with interest-only payments, on approval of credit, at prime-plus-one.

Here is the amazing feature Manulife GIF funds have: a guarantee of principal! In fact, all segregated funds have this. In brief, a segregated fund is simply a mutual fund that has been issued by a life insurance company. And it has guarantees associated with it. Traditionally, segregated funds promise a 100% guarantee over a ten-year period, which is the way the Manulife GIF works. So, if you invest $100,000 and do not take any withdrawals from it, ten years later you are guaranteed to have, at the very least, that $100,000. In other words, you are guaranteed a floor beneath your investment (and your feet). Segregated funds will guarantee the initial purchase, less any redemptions, after a ten-year period. They also give you the ability to lock in and reset this ten-year period, an opportunity that happens four or five times a year.

If your funds had a great year, and you made, say, 25%, you would want to lock that in. Let's say you re-lock your investment, now at $125,000: Ten years from now, you are 100% guaranteed to have that new, higher amount. This strategy can create a great deal of comfort for many market-fearing, market-burned investors.

This should be of particular interest, especially if you are borrowing to invest, because you must always consider the downside risks. What are the risks versus the rewards? We certainly know what the reward is: You hope to make some decent profits and get a regular, legal, solid tax reduction, by being able to write off the cost of a loan dedicated to investing. But what are your risks? Technically speaking, if you borrow to invest in a segregated fund, your only risk after a ten-year period is the interest cost that you spent — your net interest cost, after taxes. So, using our earlier $100,000 example, if you invested that amount, you paid $8,000 per year in interest over ten years. That's $80,000, which would be tax-deductible, so your net cost would have been only $40,000 over that decade.

Thus, over that ten-year period, if you borrowed to invest in a segregated fund, in a worst-case scenario you could lose $40,000 (net) — assuming that your interest rate was 8% on your loan and your marginal tax rate was 47%. There's another risk: that the interest rate of the bank will fluctuate greatly. You must be able to pay those interest costs.

Laurentian Bank's Leverage Loan

As I write this book, the Manulife loan program is the only way you can use segregated funds as collateral for a loan. However, the Laurentian Bank is working on a loan program that hopefully will be available by the time this book is published. If this program fulfills the promise of its proposal, it will be the best loan program available in Canada for mutual funds and segregated funds.

Under its proposed loan program, the Laurentian Bank will allow you to use segregated funds as collateral, guarantee in writing that there will be no margin calls, and permit you to invest in most mutual and segregated funds. As an example, if you invested $50,000 in a segregated fund, Laurentian would allow you to borrow another $50,000, which could be invested in any of a large number of mutual or segregated funds. This differs from the Manulife GIF program, in which only Manulife products can be chosen.

Match-Your-RRSP Loan

Borrowing to invest makes a lot of sense, if used conservatively. But there is another version of this strategy, which only a few investment firms in Canada offer: a match-your-RRSP loan.

Technically, you are not supposed to use your RRSP as collateral, for the mortgage on a house, or on a major car loan, or to start a new business. If you do, it is deemed a disposition of the RRSP, and tax is triggered.

But this quite fascinating concept is not set up that way (and ultimately, what happens is even better). Let me give you some examples.

Let's say that you have $10,000 in your RRSP. The investment firm will loan you an equal amount — in this case, $10,000 — to invest outside your RRSP, at very low interest-only payments (prime-plus-one). If you do not wish to put up your home or anything else as collateral, you can actually "use" your RRSP in a highly creative, legal, non-taxable fashion.

Recall what I discussed in the chapter on financial planning. Everyone should have money both inside and outside their RRSP. That is because money invested outside your RRSP is money that gives you flexibility: money for a trip, money to visit relatives, money to buy a new car or truck — whatever you want.

Alas, as I so often note, the cost of raising a family is so high (especially in tax-mad Canada) that it's usually very difficult for people to set any money aside on any kind of regular basis. As a result, other than your house — which quite often will have a large mortgage associated with it, especially when you are young — the only "real" asset most people have in their 30s or 40s is their RRSPs.

That's why I find the match-your-RRSP loan program so appealing. The companies that offer it have devised a way to allow clients to borrow money, without having to use their home as collateral, to assist them in slowly building some money outside their RRSP. And if used properly, it is an excellent strategy. It frees a house for other considerations, and, over time, you should be able to see some very good compounding taking place.

The Secured Line of Credit

Many banks and trust companies offer a secured line of credit: simply a line of credit that has collateral attached to it — usually your home. You should be able to secure the loan at prime, with interest-only payments.

This is one of the safest loans, because the bank or trust company has a solid asset as collateral, so they are not concerned with market fluctuations. Hence, there is no margin call.

Over the last few pages, I've suggested four fairly new ways to borrow to invest: the Manulife Bank Loan Program, Laurentian's proposed program, the match-your-RRSP concept, and the secured line of credit. What would make you choose one over the other?

To take advantage of the Manulife program, you'd have to have some money available outside of your RRSP, as I noted in the earlier example. If you've managed to save $25,000, Manulife would permit you to borrow up to $100,000 against that, or four-to-one. Of course, if you do not currently have any money saved outside your RRSP, you could not use the Manulife program.

With the match-your-RRSP loan program, an investment company gives you "credit" for money within your RRSP. But you do not technically use that money as collateral. You sign an agreement that states that you will not transfer your RRSP out of the company before you pay off the loan. So it's not truly being used as collateral, in the classic meaning of that term; you're simply agreeing to allow your planner to continue managing that RRSP until you pay back the loan they gave you. (It's slightly more intricate, but for the purpose of this chapter, this is how it works. If you find this an attractive idea, your financial advisor can explain it further to you.)

The secured line of credit program requires no deposit on the investor's part. However, the bank has qualifications that you must meet to qualify.

The Laurentian Bank Loan program's exact details are unfortunately unavailable in detail at this time.

What I like about each of these investment concepts is that all the organizations offering them understand that people can get a little greedy. As a result, each has taken certain precautions to help make sure that clients do not go offside, to use a fine term from the world of hockey.

In the case of the match-your-RRSP, you can invest money only in funds that the offering company has approved. The list of funds is extensive; however, they restrict the percentage you can invest in various risky funds. As an example, say you wish to be very aggressive, and you choose to buy into mutual funds such as Fidelity European or Fidelity Emerging Markets. These two would be accepted at only a 50% margin (as of this writing) and could never make up over 30% of the overall portfolio of the client.

In other words, Fidelity Investments has taken the time to figure out the actuarial numbers, so they can declare, "If you wish to invest in A, B, or C type of aggressive fund, we will permit you to put in only X amount, because we recognize that borrowing to invest can be risky." Some people may not like this, but it's set up for the protection of each client, in a way — to protect them from themselves and from the fickleness of the marketplace.

And, let's face it, we are all in business to stay in business. And the offering company wishes to make sure that, while they agree that borrowing to invest is an excellent concept, like anything in life it can be abused. If you eat too much ice cream, you will probably get a stomach ache. And if you do too much leveraging, you could go bankrupt — or at the very least, get a margin call that could put you in dire financial straits. Everything has to be done within reason.

In the case of Manulife, they, too, have their rules and regulations. If you wish to borrow from their bank, you are permitted to invest your money only in the Manulife GIF or the family of Manulife funds, specifically.

Their funds are segregated, which means they have a 100% guarantee after a ten-year period. As long as you continue to make your interest payments for ten years, your risk is really restricted to your net interest cost.

Most of these loans are demand loans, giving the lending institution the ability to "call" the loan at any time if they choose. All demand loans are treated this way.

The financial industry is continually changing. It is not unreasonable to expect that many of the terms of these loans may change. The purpose of this book is to give you an idea of some of the alternatives that are available. Make sure to review all the fine print before acting on any strategy!

RISKS, RISKS, RISKS

Think of the various kinds of risks I have discussed in this chapter and throughout this book. You could lose your job, which is one large risk. Another kind of risk is a severe drop in the market, which could lead to a margin call. (The latter is avoided pretty well, if not entirely, by the Laurentian Bank program and secured line of credit, where the chances are great that you'd never have your loan called if you are diligent in paying your monthly interest costs.)

In using the strategy of borrowing to invest, there is always the fear that "I could lose all my money!" But if you look at this strategy carefully, you can safely say to yourself, "As long as I am willing to borrow to invest in a segregated fund, make all my interest payments on time, and leave the money invested for a ten-year period, I cannot lose any of my loan. The only risk is that I will lose my net interest cost (after tax rebate)." (There is always the very slight chance that interest rates will shoot up to 15% or 17%, as they did back in the 1980s, which would be awful, but highly unlikely.)

HOW TO TAKE MONEY OUT
OF YOUR RRSP/RRIF TAX-FREE

There is one further option in the realm of borrowing to invest, and it's something very few people have ever thought about.

For this, let's go back to the Financial Plan. Remember how I suggested that a good financial plan should contain a section that shows what each year of retirement should look like, and what taxes you should expect to pay? If we go into that financial plan, and if you have been successful in saving money inside your RRSP, you'll note that the tax implications of taking money out of your RRSP/RRIF can become very significant over time.

When you are forced to take money out of your RRSP/RRIF, you are ultimately going to lose about half of your RRSP if you are at the top marginal tax bracket. It's brutal, but it's a fact of life. The rate varies from province to province, but let's use 50% tax as a good average.

Let me ask you this: What is the point of permitting your RRSP, which may be currently at say, $300,000, to grow to $700,000? When it is finally liquidated at your death, your estate will end up losing close to $350,000 to Revenue Canada.

I am not suggesting that you should not invest in RRSPs, but merely pointing out an obvious future drawback. If you have been successful in accumulating a large RRSP, or if, based on your current contribution rate, you will eventually have a large RRSP, here is a strategy for you to consider: Take money out of your RRSP/RRIF without triggering any net tax consequence, and simultaneously accumulate money outside of the RRSP, where you will earn capital gains and dividends that are taxed at a significantly lower marginal tax bracket!

The first step is to decide how quickly you want to reduce the size of your RRSP/RRIF. You would need to talk to your advisor to work out the best strategy. However, in order to keep these things simple, let's assume that you wish to reduce your RRSP by $8,000 per year. The next step is to create an offsetting tax deduction. This is accomplished by taking out a loan for investment purposes. If we assume an 8% interest rate, you would require a $100,000 loan for investment purposes in order to create the offsetting $8,000 tax deduction.

The $8,000 withdrawal from the RRSP/RRIF is taxable, while the $8,000 interest cost on the loan is tax deductible. So there is a zero net tax effect. As the investments that were purchased by the loan grow, you have successfully moved money from inside the RRSP to outside the RRSP. (This strategy would usually be implemented after you retire.)

If you are able to average 12% from your non-RRSP investment, your $100,000 loan should grow to $200,000 in six years, $400,000 in twelve years, $800,000 in eighteen years. After subtracting the loan, you would have $700,000 in less than two decades — not bad! What was your cost? If we assume that your interest cost averaged 8% a year over those eighteen years, your gross interest cost would be $144,000. Don't forget, this interest cost has been tax deductible. Assuming a 50% marginal tax bracket, your net, out-of-pocket cost was only $72,000. This translates into more than a nine-times increase in your money over eighteen years. (Also not bad!)

Remember, you did take $144,000 out of your RRSP/RRIF to pay for the interest cost. So an argument could be made that your real cost was $144,000 and not $72,000. My feeling is that you were going to lose half of your RRSP in taxes on withdrawal anyway, so I believe the $72,000 is more accurate. Ultimately, however, it really doesn't matter. This strategy looks good both ways.

As in all strategies, there are risks, but we've seen earlier that they can be reduced by investing the loaned money in a segregated fund, which will guarantee your principal (the original $100,000) after a ten-year period, or upon death.

The worst-case scenario would be zero gain on your $100,000 loan over a ten-year period, so you would lose $72,000. You have to ask yourself how likely this is to occur. If the money is invested conservatively, the risk would be exceptionally low.

Do not forget that the $700,000 capital gain is taxable, so about $262,500 would have to be paid to Revenue Canada in capital gains tax when it was sold.

Still, a $72,000 net interest cost after tax deduction, which grows to approximately $437,500 after tax over eighteen years is more than a six-times increase in your money, which I find quite acceptable.

As an investor, you would need to average a little over 6% on your investment to break even. Now, what are the chances that you will earn 6%-plus per year over an eighteen-year period?

Most advisors warn their clients not to take out any loans, because they are so expensive, and so costly to keep paying for. But when it comes to borrowing to invest, I suggest that it's far more expensive not to make this simple, sensible, logical, safe financial move.

CHAPTER NINE

The Family Tax Strategy

O ne welcome problem that sometimes emerges in financial planning — and it is most assuredly a welcome
problem to have — is that clients have been fortunate enough
to accumulate money both inside and outside their RRSP. And
have, as well, grown to realize that they are most likely not
going to be able to spend it all.

The questions arise: What should you do with this money?
How do you maintain control of it, without giving it all to the
kids? And what if you don't have any kids? What is the best
tax-sheltered investment to make in situations like this?

My solution is something called a Family Tax Strategy (FTS):
a great idea whose time has definitely come. The Family Tax
Strategy is a name I have given to a Universal Life Insurance
product marketed by most insurance companies. These products range from excellent to poor, so before purchasing one,
make sure you talk to an independent agent who represents
more than one company.

The FTS is one of the finest, most rewarding tax-deferral
systems available in Canada today. But you have to be very
careful to choose one that will serve your needs superbly for
many, many years.

Why such concern? Because once you establish your FTS,

your money is more or less locked in for life. Let's look at a bit of history before we go any further. Two acts cover taxation in Canada — the Bank Act and the Insurance Act. Most Canadians are aware of the Bank Act (it's the act that dictates how much tax we pay on dividends, interest, and capital gains and the investments that yield these incomes). The Insurance Act has a couple of huge advantages that the banks would *love* to have. Remember back in the mid-1990s, when the banks were complaining vociferously about how the insurance companies had so many advantages? Then, suddenly, you didn't hear these complaints any more.

Guess what? The banks have been busy either buying insurance companies like mad or setting up their own. Banks are not fools, and they recognize a tactical advantage. The banks are hoping to offer the types of products to their clients that insurance companies sell.

What advantages do insurance companies have that make the banks lust after them? First, if you save money within an insurance policy, it is creditor-proof. There are certain limitations on this feature, and as the years go by, the court may refine such advantages, so you cannot assume they will last forever. But generally speaking, if you have saved money inside a life insurance policy, whether it is an RRSP investment or a non-RRSP investment, and you subsequently go bankrupt, the money in the life insurance policy is usually held to be creditor-proof. (Traditionally, the number given is two years before the bankruptcy. If you have held the life insurance investment for less than two years, you may be called upon to prove that you had no prior knowledge that you were having financial problems.)

Second, when you save money inside a life insurance policy, it compounds completely tax deferred. That's right — exactly the same way that money does inside an RRSP. The FTS has a list of eligible investments that you can choose from or move between without triggering tax. These include indexes such as the Nasdaq, Standard and Poor, S&P 500, Toronto Stock Exchange 100, etc. A full line of GICs are also available.

Say you owned as an investment Templeton Growth, one of the great mutual fund success stories of the past few decades. And you decided one day that you wanted to move it into Templeton International stock. Let's assume that you had originally invested $10,000 in Templeton Growth, and doubled that to $20,000 in five years.

When you switched from one fund to the other, you'd have a $10,000 capital gain, so 25% of that — $2,500 — would be tax free. And the other $7,500 in profit would have to be listed in your total income of that year. If you were at the top tax bracket that year, you would have to pay $3,750 in income tax on that profit — on average, about 50%. (The rate will vary somewhat by province.)

But what happens if you want to move money from fund to fund or from one equity to another inside the FTS? Or what happens inside your life insurance policy, if you choose to move your investment from one equity to another? In either case, you do not trigger any tax whatsoever.

THIS IS WORTH A CLOSER LOOK!

Look at the chart on the following page. By referring to it as you read through this chapter, you can compare an equity mutual fund to an RRSP and an FTS.

Money put into an FTS is after tax, of course, so you don't get any tax deductions. That is the great advantage that an RRSP has — the money you put into it is tax deductible. If you invest money in mutual funds, stocks, etc., outside of your RRSP, it is, sadly, also not tax deductible.

The money in your RRSP grows tax deferred, and regardless of the investment you have made, you are free to move your money around inside your plan without triggering any tax.

Although the money you deposit for investment in your Family Tax Strategy is not tax deductible, the increase in value

COMPARISON — RRSP, EQUITY MUTUAL FUNDS, AND FTS

	RRSP	EQUITY MUTUAL FUNDS	FTS
Investment	Tax deductible	Not deductible	Not deductible
Growth	Tax deferred	Tax deferred	Tax deferred
Income	Taxable as high as 45.6% (Alberta)	Taxable as high as 34.2% (Alberta)	Tax free
Death of Spouse #1	Tax-free transfer	Tax-free transfer	Tax-free transfer
Death of Spouse #2	Taxable as high as 45.6%	Taxable as high as 34.2%	Tax-free transfer
Creditor Proof	No	No	Yes
Contribution Limits	The lesser of $13,500 or 18% of earned income	No restrictions	No restrictions

once it's inside the plan is completely tax deferred! You pay no tax on interest, and you trigger no tax if you choose to move money from one investment to another. In short, you get total tax deferral inside your FTS, just as you do inside an RRSP.

What happens, then, if you want an income stream? When you eventually take money out of your RRSP, it is taxed at the very height of your marginal tax bracket at the time. This could be close to 50%, or even more, depending on the province where you reside and your taxable income at the time you take the money out.

The gains withdrawn from equity mutual funds or stocks can be taxed as high as 35%. But money redeemed from the FTS is tax free if the plan is set up properly.

Some things remain the same, of course. In the case of an RRSP, with the death of Spouse #1, the RRSP is transferred to Spouse #2. In the case of an FTS, the death of Spouse #1 also shifts the FTS to Spouse #2. Ditto with a mutual fund if it is registered as joint with the sole rights of survivor.

With the death of Spouse #2, all RRSPs become taxable — and, of course, the estate pays the taxes before any money goes to the beneficiaries. The only way around this expense is to either spend the money while you're alive or purchase life insurance to cover the taxes. But the money *still* goes to Revenue Canada; you're simply replacing what you should be paying with the tax-free proceeds of an insurance policy.

And how about your FTS? The FTS pays out 100% tax free to your stated beneficiaries — *outside of probate*. (Compare that to an equity mutual fund or a stock held in your name: The proceeds from a sale are taxable, with only the first 25% tax free; the balance is brought into your taxable income.)

In summary: With an FTS, the investment is made with after-tax dollars; the money grows tax deferred; a tax-free income or lump sum can be taken out; on the death of Spouse #1 the FTS goes to Spouse #2; on the death of Spouse #2, it goes completely tax free to the stated beneficiaries outside of probate. The lawyers don't get their hands on any of it! In addition, it is creditor protected, so if you go bankrupt, the creditors cannot get their sticky little hands on it, either.

Let's say that you are a government employee. You suddenly get downsized (which is hardly a shocking or unusual situation, nowadays). You decide to set up your own in-house business. Alas, you end up going bankrupt. If you have been putting money into a normal RRSP, you can lose it to creditors, along with any non-registered investments. Yet an FTS is creditor-protected! (We will talk about creditor protection and RRSPs in Chapter Twelve.)

I must make it perfectly clear that FTSs are longer-term investments. Redemption fees last about a decade, and those fees are fairly significant over the first couple of years. Furthermore, you must be insurable.

The Benefits of the FTS

1. Investment growth, including interest, is tax deferred.
2. Investment selections can be changed without triggering income tax.
3. An annual income, tax free, is available for retirement or for other financial objectives.
4. Tax-free income can reduce social security–benefits clawbacks.
5. Estate values are increased substantially on a tax-free basis.
6. A generation of income tax can be skipped by insuring an offspring.

The Basic Strategy Behind the
Family Tax Strategy (or FTS)

A. Set up a regular investment that goes into an FTS on a monthly or annual basis.
B. Once the money is inside the FTS, all the income earned grows tax free; you can change your investment selections at any time without triggering income tax.

C. The accumulated fund within the FTS will establish the basis for an annual income. Rather than redeeming this money directly from the FTS, you will use the FTS as collateral for a bank loan, which is advanced to you in installments each year, making the annual income fully tax free. Interest payments on the loan will be capitalized, so that you won't have to pay them; you increase the loan each year by the amount borrowed, plus the accumulated interest.

D. The insurance portion of the plan is set up on a joint second-to-die basis. Upon the death of Spouse #1, the plan continues with Spouse #2. When the remaining spouse dies, there is a death benefit payable, which is completely tax free. The loan is paid off from the proceeds and the balance flows tax free to your estate or heirs outside of probate.

HOW DOES MONEY COME OUT OF AN FTS TAX FREE?

To take the money out of the FTS tax free, we simply use it as collateral for a loan. If the investments in the FTS are GICs, you can borrow up to 90% of the value of the plan. (I do not recommend borrowing more than 80%.)

When you borrow money from a bank, the loan is not taxable. The FTS is treated exactly the same way. The bank will permit you to borrow money monthly to create an income, or as a lump sum, whichever you prefer. Think of it as a line of credit, using the FTS as collateral. Interest payments on the loan are capitalized, so you do not have to pay them. This means that each year or month, you borrow to give yourself an income, as well as borrow to pay the interest cost on the loan.

"Okay, then," you now mumble, "but depending upon how much I borrow from the bank this way, twenty or twenty-five years from now, I might owe a million dollars! And for that, I'll have to earn two million dollars — paying one million to

Revenue Canada, to have one million dollars left to pay off this loan! That sure doesn't sound very good, does it?"

The idea of compounding interest costs and debt can be intimidating. It should be understood that you are *not* required to take money out of the plan in this fashion. You can simply redeem money. A portion of the redemption would be considered return of capital (tax free) and the balance would be taxed as interest income.

As long as your investment return averages the same return as your interest rate (hopefully it will be higher), the loan strategy for redemptions works well. Also remember that upon the second spouse's death, the Family Tax Strategy pays out tax free. The accumulated loan would therefore be paid off with tax-free dollars, rather than after-tax dollars. You would need only $1 million in the plan to pay off a $1 million loan (not $2 million).

AN EXAMPLE OF AN FTS
VERSUS REGULAR INVESTMENT

Let's look at a husband and wife, both age 40 and non-smokers. They invest $5,000 per year for five years and then leave that money to compound until they reach the age of 65, when they will start to take out an income of $15,000 a year, after tax. What would be the after-tax difference between investing inside an FTS and investing as they would regularly? To keep things equal, we will assume an 8.2% rate of return for both the regular investment and the FTS. For tax purposes we will use a 46% marginal tax bracket, and assume that 8.2% return is interest income and the growth is taxed every year for the purpose of withdrawing money from the FTS. We will also assume an 8% loan rate.

If you turn to Appendix Six, you will see that the regular investment (non-FTS) grew to a high of $64,972 after tax in year 24, when the husband and wife were 64. The $15,000 after-tax withdrawals began in year 25 and were sustained for four years. In the fifth year, only $13,163 was left to withdraw.

Under the same scenario, the FTS (NN Challenger Universal Life product, in this case) accumulated a cash value of $153,413 in year 24, and had $285,185 worth of life insurance included. If both spouses were to die at this time, the estate would receive $438,598 tax free, as opposed to $64,972 after tax with the regular investment.

With the regular investment, in year 25 the couple started to take the $15,000 yearly income out after tax via the loan process described earlier. In year 28, when the regular investment ran out of money (with a little over $13,000 left), the FTS had an estate value, after paying off the loan, of $482,979, of which $153,154 was cash value. (The difference is life insurance.) If you continue with the FTS example, you will see that the couple should be able to keep taking out the $15,000 annually as long as they live and still have an estate value left upon the second spouse's death.

The tax-free estate difference between the two strategies is $469,816 after twenty-nine years. Only $25,000 has been invested into the FTS over five years, yet the FTS has an after-tax estate advantage of nearly half a million dollars over the regular investment, after a $60,000 redemption in both strategies.

For the purpose of this example, we have treated the income as interest income. If capital gains were earned, this would make the regular investment look a little better, as capital gains growth is tax deferred and is taxed at a lower rate than is interest. The Universal Life policy (FTS) would *still* look significantly better, though, as its growth is completely tax deferred. If we had assumed a higher rate of return for both alternatives, the Universal Life Insurance program (FTS) would have looked even better by comparison.

You end up with more money when you put your investing dollars into an FTS instead of a traditional investment such as stocks or equity-based mutual funds. You'll have more compounding, and so, more money to spend after tax. Your actual income will depend on how your investment has grown for both examples. The greater the growth, the larger the potential income. You will also wind up with many hundreds of thousands of dollars in life insurance!

The life insurance, by the way, is essentially free. We know that nothing in life is free, but the tax-free compounding that you will make on your money inside your FTS will be *more* than enough to pay for the cost of your insurance — and will leave you ahead of traditional investments such as mutual funds. You now have hundreds of thousands of dollars that have accumulated tax free. You can take out a tax-free lump sum or create an income stream. Upon the second spouse's death, any money not spent (after paying off the loan) will flow tax free to the stated beneficiaries outside of probate. The tax-free income or lump sum that you can take from the FTS will not affect your marginal tax brackets and thus will not create a clawback situation on any of your pensions.

If you are likely to have a tax problem due to large RRSPs or a large increase in the property value of a cottage, rental income properties, or even investment growth, the insurance in the Universal Life policy will now cover some or all of the taxes on your estate.

Elderly people especially can benefit from a plan such as this. We have found that, generally, people tend to stop travelling to a great extent by the time they reach their mid-80s. Their bones are a bit more brittle, they fear breaking a leg or a hip, they aren't comfortable sitting for long periods of time, and they just prefer to be in familiar surroundings. As a result, many elderly men and women find that their income requirements tend to be quite a bit lower in their last decade or two than in their middle ones. Rather suddenly, money starts accumulating, usually in their bank accounts.

If you were an elderly person with an FTS, why wouldn't you simply stop taking money out, and start putting money back in — and have it compound tax free? (That sure beats the

3% to 4% on a GIC, or the 1% to 2% on those miserable "investment builders"/savings accounts that most banks were offering in the last months of the twentieth century!)

What you have, in effect, is a plan that is fully legal and that allows you to put money in and/or take money out, tax free. If you are putting the money in, it compounds tax free.

HOW DO YOU GO ABOUT PURCHASING AN **FTS?**

In fact, the Family Tax Strategy is simply a Universal Life Insurance policy. To set one up, you must be insurable. But here lies the problem. This is a long-term situation — you are considering going to bed with a life insurance company for what could be twenty-five, maybe even fifty years.

There is a huge difference between Universal Life products! There are a number of variables you should look at. First is the cost of this insurance. Second are the investment alternatives you can choose from. (You are restricted to the investments that they offer.) And, of course, third are the expenses charged by the company for doing all this miraculous work for you.

Most plans say "The insurance is guaranteed." But you have to read the fine print to see what the actual cost is, as compared to other companies.

As discussed earlier, there is a large difference between insurance companies' products and prices. It is best to ask your independent agent for at least three examples of the same product offered by different companies. This is especially true for Universal Life's insurance policies. You are talking about a long-term commitment, and the redemption fees are large if you choose incorrectly the first time.

I have looked into the insurance costs of $400,000 of term-to-100 life insurance for a female non-smoker who is 66 years of age. (Term-to-100 insurance is pure insurance that is guaranteed to keep the same premium costs for life.) The cheapest payment was $9,287 a year and one of the more expensive ones was $12,832 a year. That's a $3,545-a-year difference for the same product! It's not surprising that the older you are, the more expensive the insurance will be. It is also logical that as the insured gets older, the actuarial numbers should be more exact, so you would expect a smaller difference between companies.

Remember, insurance is sold, not bought. Be careful — and shop around.

When you introduce a savings element to your insurance plan (i.e., Universal Life), you can clearly see how it is even easier for life insurance companies to hide costs and extra expenses, especially when they're spread over a long period of time. These expenses can add up.

As soon as you get a product that is all wrapped up in a box, with a nice red bow on top, the chances are you'll be paying far more than if you had purchased the individual components. You must be very, very careful and compare at least three companies on an apples-to-apples basis.

In this example of the Family Tax Strategy, I have used the NN Challenger, which is a Universal Life product. One of the reasons that money grows inside the Universal Life products faster than outside is that many of the companies have bonuses that are paid out at different periods over and above the investment return that you earn.

If you average over an 8% return in the NN Challenger after five years, you receive an extra 1.75% bonus added to your return. This continues as long as your return averages over 8%. If you average less than 8%, the bonus is 1.25% a year.

INTERGENERATIONAL TAX-FREE TRANSFER OF WEALTH

The purpose of the FTS is to have money compound free of personal income tax. If you want money, it can be taken out free of tax via a loan that is not repaid until the death of the insured. Investments inside the FTS can be adjusted without triggering tax. In short, look at the FTS as an *investment product*, rather than as a way of purchasing insurance.

If you are not insurable, you cannot be the insured. However, this does not prevent you from being the owner of the plan. There are four important components: the insured, the owner, the contingent owner, and the beneficiary. The plan itself compounds tax free until the insured dies. Then it pays out tax free to the beneficiary. However, the owner of the plan is in full control. He or she controls the cash within the plan. The insured and the owner can be the same person, but they are not required to be.

Because many wealthy Canadians are looking at ways of creating and preserving an estate for as long as possible, I would like to suggest a way you may not have thought of. What would happen if you purchased a Family Tax Strategy (Universal Life policy) and had a grandchild as the insured, you as the owner, and your offspring as the contingent owner? If your grandchild was fortunate enough to enjoy a long healthy life — say, to age 90 — you could create or preserve a very large estate.

The money you put into the plan could compound for ninety years if the plan was taken out at your grandchild's birth and the money was not spent by the owners (the grandparent, then the parent, and finally the insured). The life insurance would pass tax free to your grandchild's child. Theoretically, there could be a transfer of money from the first generation to the fourth generation, free of personal income tax.

As this type of plan becomes more popular in the years ahead — possibly spurred on by books like this one — Universal Life policies may not continue to exist in the same format. But if you enter into an agreement that is legal at the time, and done in good faith, the government cannot go back and make it retroactively illegal (known as a grandfather clause). Although you are well advised to think through your strategies carefully, don't put off acting too long in case some of these advantages are legislated away.

YOU CRAFTY, INTELLIGENT, LEGAL TAX AVOIDER, YOU!

You have now set up a trust, which grows completely tax deferred. The insurance company is taxed, a bit, on the gains; so there is *some* tax, which must be paid.

The important thing is that you don't have to pay these taxes at your top marginal tax bracket, and neither does your family. If you don't need the money, this is a superb system for protecting your money from tax and allowing it to grow.

You have to remember that all of the cash inside the plan pays out. As does all of the life insurance death benefit, of course. This is not like the old "whole life" programs, where you received either/or. You get both here. It is one thing to know that you are going to leave some money, whether for your children or grandchildren. But there are some other issues to deal with. Do you want to leave a percentage in cash that they can receive on your death and use, in whatever manner they want? Your offspring are going to be forced to save over the long term, correct? Then wouldn't it be best to leave them a tax shelter?

In these situations, I recommend that you set up a Family Tax Shelter for each offspring with the offspring as the insured. In your will, state, "The kids cannot cash this in or take any money out of it, or even use it as collateral, until the age of 50" (or 60 or whatever age you choose). Suddenly, your children and grandchildren will never have to worry about their retirement — and you won't have to worry about their retirement! As long as you, the owner, are alive, you can do what you wish. When you die, the codicils in the will state your wishes. (There is no provision for this in the Universal Life product, so you would have to make arrangements with your executor or lawyer.)

It would be unrealistic not to address the issues that arise if one of your children divorces. Say your married son is the insured, and you are the owner of the FTS. The FTS is deemed the owner's asset. Therefore, if your son or daughter goes through a divorce, the now-former in-law would not be entitled to any of the money in a divorce proceeding. This holds true even if your son put money into the FTS as well.

If you look at the compounding numbers, depending on the age of the children or grandchildren, even $10,000 or $20,000, left for thirty or forty years, will accumulate into a sizeable amount of money. Each insured would have his or her own policy with the parent or grandparent as the owner.

You may be concerned that the cost of a permanent insurance policy, as opposed to straight-term, will be incredibly expensive. In a Universal Life Insurance policy, you can choose whether the insurance component is annual renewable term (which is the cheapest form of insurance you can buy), or whether it is term-to-100. And even when you've made a decision, you can change it later if you so choose.

Chapter Ten

The Attractive Concept of Systematic Withdrawal Plans

When I look at my own retirement — and I am barely into my 40s — I think in terms of how much money I'll need to have invested in mutual funds to give me a reasonable income. How will I get this income? Dividend rates and interest rates are fairly low, and it's not easy to live off a 3% or 4% return. Ultimately, you are going to have to live off the capital appreciation.

Once I retire, I will probably not want to fiddle with my investments too much. In fact, I don't like moving them around a lot right now! I have found that most of my retired clients are looking for something that is fairly easy, and that they "don't have to look at every day." They want to be hands-off, and understandably so.

When you reach your 60s and beyond, you begin to realize that life does not go on forever. You bury friends, relatives, co-workers, warm acquaintances. And you start to be sensitive to, and respect, the value (and fleetingness) of time. To most young people, time has no real relation to or meaning for them; when they talk long term, that long term may well be the Thursday after next.

But when you start getting older — around the age of retirement, give or take a few years — you recognize that you have indeed turned a corner; that you must find time to enjoy your surroundings more. You want to travel, visit loved ones, smell the roses, and so on. I noted earlier in this book that when both spouses come to a financial advisor, it's usually one more than the other who is *really* interested in investments and how they work. I always hope that this more-interested spouse will set up the portfolio in such a manner that if something happened to him or her, the surviving spouse would not have to worry about any details, but could just leave the investments as they were and let them grow.

This is why the Systematic Withdrawal Plan — the SWP — was created. It is one of the best tools around, as long as you are comfortable with mutual funds and having some exposure to equities.

What makes the SWP so attractive? First, it gives you a regular income that is deposited directly into your bank — whether monthly, quarterly, semi-annually, or annually.

But far more important is the way that our good friends at Revenue Canada look at it. The SWP is *incredibly* tax efficient; it tends to skew the tax on your investments into the future and gives you a large percentage of the income that you receive "at the beginning," which is usually considered by Revenue Canada to be "return of capital."

What this means is that it is tax free. If you have put your own money in, the government can't tax you when you take your own money out; they can tax only the capital gains, dividends, and interest you earn from that investment.

A CHART TO TREASURE

You can set up an SWP on essentially any mutual fund. Usually the only restriction is that you must have at least $10,000 in a specific fund before you begin to withdraw money in this fashion. This seems only logical, because if you had only, say, $1,000 invested, and you began to take 10% a year from it, this would be a grand total of $100 a year — divided by twelve equal monthly installments — meaning that you are taking out a mere $8.33 a month.

One of the best charts to show how an SWP works is the one put out by Trimark. With their kind permission, I have included their chart, which shows how an SWP has worked with that very successful mutual fund, in Appendix Seven. At Trimark's request, I will remind you that the "Trimark Fund SWP chart for the period ending December 31, 1998 is provided as a general illustration of Systematic Withdrawal Plans by Trimark Investment Management Inc. The Fund's past performance is not necessarily indicative of future results, as unit value and investment returns will fluctuate. Please read your prospectus carefully before investing in any mutual fund, or setting up a SWP."

I should note right off the bat that SWPs are designed for money outside your RRSP, not inside it. As we all know so well, when you take money out of an RRSP, the proceeds are fully taxable. The benefit should be clear, then: This is tax-preferred income we are describing here.

With an SWP, you can invest in, say, international funds. Over the long term, since Canada accounts for a mere 3% of the world's stock market capitalization, you tend to get greater returns abroad.

Looking at the Trimark Fund SWP chart, you can see that it begins on September 1, 1981. Along the top of this chart, you see the total annual withdrawals, the return of capital, the capital gain or loss, the cumulative total withdrawals, and the dividends, which are reinvested.

Then, you see the account value of the Trimark Fund, followed by a comparison with a GIC or a term deposit that has been returning 8%. The chart assumes that the owner of the plan — let's say it was you — started at the 40% marginal tax bracket. (If you are at a higher tax bracket, this entire SWP concept will look even better!)

In this example, you began with $100,000, and there was a

4% front-end load fee, paid off the top. This was the only way that you could purchase mutual funds, back in the early 1980s; there was no such thing as a Deferred Sales Charge. (When you purchase a mutual fund on a DSC basis, it means that all your money goes in and begins to work its magic, with only a declining redemption fee on the back end.)

You are allowed to withdraw 10% a year, without triggering the redemption fee that usually lasts about eight years. The fee generally starts at 5.5% and declines to zero in the eighth year. See a simplified prospectus for each fund's specific schedule. As I just noted, when you take money out using this plan, a good portion of it is considered "return of capital." Let me explain how that works:

Let's say you purchased a farm that consisted of ten acres at a cost of $1,000 per acre. Think of it as ten $1,000 chunks. For the sake of this analogy, we'll say the farm increases in value by 20%. Each of those acres is now worth $1,200, so you decide you want to have an income from this property. If you decide to subdivide the farm and sell a one-acre lot, how will the money you receive for the sale be treated, tax-wise?

Since you had originally paid $1,000 for that acre, the $1,000 you get back would be considered return of capital — or, in other words, it would be judged by Revenue Canada to be the refund of the original money you used to purchase it. This is, of course, non-taxable. (When you look at the SWP column, and see the Return of Capital listing, that is what that means.)

You have also had a $200 capital gain. The first 25% of a capital gain is tax free. The next $150 of your profit from that sale is taxable. If you are at the top marginal tax bracket, you would "lose" $75 to the government in taxes, assuming a 50% marginal tax rate.

Therefore, you received $1,125 after tax from the sale of the one-acre parcel of land, which you are now free to spend. What did you pay in tax? You paid only $75 (assuming that top marginal tax bracket). Not bad, is it — to receive $1,125 and pay only $75 in tax on such earnings!

Look at your farm today. What do you have left? The farm is still worth $10,800, even though you have sold that one acre of land; in other words, it is still worth $800 more than you paid for it, not counting the withdrawal.

An SWP is designed to give you a tax-preferred income, while still permitting the original investment to grow.

The Trimark illustration underlines the beauty of mutual funds. Mutual funds are, unlike farms, easily subdividable — so you can cash out one share, or a handful of shares, if you so desire. This is a huge advantage over a common stock. Recall, when you own common stocks, you have to sell what is called a "board lot." So you have to sell a minimum amount, whether you really want to or not; for this, you would pay a reasonable commission. But if you sell an "odd lot" (say four-teen shares, or thirty-nine, or sixty-five, because that's how much money you needed at that moment), the commission you must pay shoots up dramatically.

The mutual fund, on the other hand, gives you wonderful flexibility; you can take out any amount you wish — and on a monthly basis — and not be hit by endless and frequent bro-kerage fees, as you would with the selling of common stocks.

You can be sure — 100% certain, in fact — that there will be years when the value of your investment will drop, and you will lose money. That is the way it is with equities, whether they are bought individually or through a mutual fund; they are different than GICs and T-bills and various types of bonds, as I've discussed before. There are few guarantees in life.

The Rental Property from Heaven

Here's another example I like to use. Imagine that you owned a rental income property, and you had tenants from heaven (not at all like the classic image of the "tenants from hell"). You never had to put a single penny more into the property, as these angelic folk do all their own painting, wallpapering, plumbing repairs, everything. And they always pay on the first of each month, never missing a payment — and they always bring the full amount of their rent to you, right to your door; you never have to run after them, or worry if their cheque might bounce.

Would you be concerned by the inevitable fluctuations in the home's value over the years? After all, you know that every single month, that rent cheque will be paid. We all know, if you own a house, you'll go through good housing markets, bad housing markets, and mediocre ones. Your only concern should arise when you are planning to sell your house; at that time, you would be following the ups and downs of the housing market closely.

Most people think of a rental income house as having permanence, don't they? They can see the building, touch it, even feel it. While a stock or a mutual fund is simply a piece of paper, you must learn to think of your mutual fund account (and your SWP) in the same way as you would think of that rental house. Imagine that your rent cheque is forever being handed to you, happily, on the first of every month, while your rental house (that is, the lump sum of your mutual fund investment) fluctuates each year. You may check it occasionally, to make sure the numbers are correct on the cheque, and you might wish to occasionally note, in passing, how your house is doing in terms of the marketplace, but you don't really worry about it. And why should you?

This is how the SWP works. Let's go through the Trimark chart of an SWP in Appendix Seven a line at a time, to see just how marvellous this concept is.

A Line-by-Line Look at a
Systematic Withdrawal Plan in Action

Starting in October 1981, you began to take out $833.33 every month. Your total withdrawals were $2,500 for that first period, which ran only three months, from the end of September to the end of December. Of that, the "return of capital" was considered to be $2,559. That is more than you took out. Uh-oh, you think: there was a capital loss there; you actually lost a little bit of money. These are cumulative withdrawals, and what you took out first was $2,500.

That year, Trimark paid out no distributions, and because there was a small loss, there was no tax liability. Hence, you were able to spend that $2,500 in any way you and your family chose, and you had to pay absolutely no tax.

Now, look at the Trimark Fund account value at the end of that first year, and you will notice that the value of the investment actually went up (from that original $96,000, since $4,000 was lopped off at the beginning to pay the commission to the person who set up the plan); it's now worth $98,594.

The next year, you withdrew over the full twelve months, and since the amount is $833.33 each month, over that entire year you received $10,000 in your bank account on the SWP from Trimark. Of that amount, fully $9,567 was considered return of capital! So you had a capital gain of a mere $433; your cumulative withdrawals from your original $100,000 account (actually $96,000) have been $10,000, plus the $2,500 from those last three months of 1981. Trimark, as you see, paid a distribution of $1,350 that year, so you had a total tax liability of $426. In this example and for most SWPs, the distributions are reinvested. However, you have to pay the tax that is triggered.

So, in 1982 you received $10,000 to spend and had to pay only $426 in taxes. If you had received that $10,000 in interest payments from a GIC you purchased, you would have had to pay $4,000 in tax to the government (assuming 40% marginal taxes), as opposed to this magical SWP from Trimark, where you had to pay only $426 on similar "earnings."

Notice how, on the chart, the numbers keep growing. Furthermore, you will quickly see that, if you look at the annual tax liability column on the chart, generally speaking, you pay less tax with the SWP than you do with the "interest-earning investment" on the other side.

True, there are several periods, such as in 1990, where you had to pay $8,340 in income tax. But then, you did receive a $24,894 dividend that year, so what can you expect? If you make money, you have to pay a little bit of tax. And don't forget, this portfolio is now worth $207,814 — since it began at $100,000, it has more than doubled in value. (And check those GICs, as listed on the chart — they are worth only $69,880 at this point, not even half of what the Trimark Fund has achieved. And you still had to pay $2,206 in taxes on the return from the GICs, so you can see how much better the mutual fund has done.)

It's True — Mutual Funds Do Fluctuate

Let's look at the Trimark Fund account value over the years; it is quite informative. You started off, as you recall, with $96,000 — already in the hole! — because of the $4,000 acquisition fee, back in 1981. (Remember, this fee is no longer required.) It quickly grew to $98,594, then to $122,658, and then to $155,045. Then, uh-oh, it dropped to $146,443!

How horrible! The Trimark Fund account has dropped $8,602 in value! But to complain about that is as silly as getting depressed after finding a twenty-dollar bill on the street, and then having a loonie or two roll out of your pocket when you bend over to pick it up. Should you rejoice over the found $20 or bemoan the lost $2? I think the answer is pretty clear that you should be more happy than sad. After all, you took out $10,000 that same year in Systematic Withdrawals, did you not?

Many a client will rush to the financial advisor at a time like that and begin to wonder if he or she made the right decision. Let's hope that the advisor tells the client, "I urge you to just hold on; you're in this for the long term; don't panic over a tiny bit of spilt milk, when the cow is in such great health!"

Look what happened *then*, following the chart along. It moved back up to $189,115, then further up, to $199,525. Ooops — then it dropped to $185,303, this time a loss of $14,222. That's a lot of money, and readers who are over the age of 40 may remember when they worked an entire year in order to earn $14,222 or less!

Yes, it's possible that many thousands of clients who held Trimark Fund weren't too keen about this fund that particular year. But let's see what happened if they held on. Soon it goes up to $241,192 in value! Oh, yes, it drops down to $207,814 that year, a walloping $33,378 loss — more than the fund made in many years. But what happened then? Why, it continued to climb, and climb, and climb.

You want a guarantee in life? I'll give you one: I can guarantee 100% that every two to five years, certainly every three to five years, you are going to lose *some* money, whether in stocks, bonds, or mutual funds. That's the nature of the beast. Recall the worst crashes in the market — 1987, 1990, the summer of 1998 (if not the fall). There will always be years in which people lose money, whether in mutual funds or in common stocks.

Yet the worst possible thing anyone could do would be to sell at that point. And if you are the type who panics and wants to sell with every bump, burp, or belch in the market, you should *not* enter into a Systematic Withdrawal Plan in the first place; you should buy a Back-to-Back (described in Chapter Fourteen), which is (at least) always better than a GIC.

However, if you have the fortitude to treat a mutual-fund holding, and an SWP, like a rental income property (with those great tenants-from-heaven that you've got living there), and hold your funds for the long term, you should be well-rewarded.

More Thoughts About Your Systematic Withdrawal Plan
When you look over the history of SWPs — especially with quality mutual funds like Trimark's — you can see that the

Systematic Withdrawal Plan has worked incredibly well. But if you are even the slightest bit concerned about or wary of this concept, here is a modest suggestion. Whether you put in $10,000 or $100,000 or $1,000,000, don't take out any regular income in the first year, as you see was done on this Trimark chart.

I recommend to my clients that they "wait out" the entire first year after they invest and begin an SWP; allow the fund to grow a little bit before starting to withdraw money from it. After all, the worst that could possibly happen would be to take out 10% one year, and then have a 20% loss that year — it's certainly possible — and find your not-so-grand total down fully 30% — nearly one-third. That would be enough to scare many an investor away.

So leave the money in for at least the first full year after deposit (two years, if possible). Give it a chance to grow, as it probably will.

Remember: This chart is not a computer-generated projection. It is a demonstration of what actually happened with the Trimark Fund!

Notice that, over a sixteen-year period, if you invested $100,000 on September 1, 1981, by December 31, 1997, you have taken out (systematically withdrawn) a sum just shy of $162,500. Not bad. You still have $671,799 left in your fund. That's over two-thirds of a million dollars in your investment plan, up rather impressively from $100,000, in a mere sixteen years. And you've been taking out $10,000 every year, most of it taxed very lightly.

What is the catch? Well, as you know, over time inflation will slash away at purchasing power; look in the back of your kitchen cupboard at the prices on older cans of tuna or baked beans, and you will know precisely what I'm getting at. So, unless you want to leave a lot of money to your children, you may wish to increase the amount you take out in your regular withdrawals.

You can see just how attractive a Systematic Withdrawal Plan can be:

- It provides you with a steady income.
- It will dip into capital (if need be) if the investment is down.
- It provides you with a tax-advantaged way of taking money out of your savings.
- It defers taxes until well into the future.
- It provides protection against inflation, by beating inflation most, if not all, of the time.
- The money can be deposited directly into your bank account on a monthly, quarterly, semi-annual, annual, or even bi-monthly basis.
- You can turn it off or on at any time.
- You can make additions to it, or take lump sums out.

In short, the Systematic Withdrawal Plan is incredibly flexible, and, in my opinion, it is one of the best strategies for retired people. Those who wish to have an income from their investments, but with an eye to keeping their taxes to a minimum, will benefit as well.

But — and I cannot stress this enough — any SWP you set up does fluctuate, like anything that involves equities and mutual funds. And when it fluctuates, you absolutely and resolutely must not sell; if you do, you'll end up losing.

As you know, the maximum you can take out, without incurring any redemption fees on a DSC fund, is 10%. I recommend that people start withdrawing at a lower rate of perhaps 6% or 7% each time for two reasons. First, you want to give your money and your investment time to grow. Second, you will still do better with an SWP than with a GIC — the SWP is tax-advantaged so it's going to leave you in a far better position than other kinds of investments.

Choose a mutual fund that is involved with international equities. This gives the money manager the maximum amount of flexibility, and ensures that you go into it, and hold, for the long term.

Here's why investing for the long term is so important: Let's assume that you've invested $10,000 and that it has grown to $20,000 (by the way, this analogy isn't true only in the case of a Systematic Withdrawal Plan; it's true for any investment). Now you've decided that the market is high, and you're concerned that a serious correction is on the horizon. So you want to move the money into bonds or cash — in other words, move it sideways.

What would be the implication of this move? Of that $20,000, fully $10,000 would be refund of capital. The other $10,000 is your capital gain. And of that, one-fourth, or $2,500, would be tax free. But $7,500 would be taxable. So at a 50% marginal tax rate, you would lose in the range of $3,750 to income tax. You have just lost a little under 20% of your $20,000 in taxes. By comparison, when you made that market-timing decision to sell your investment, your portfolio (or the stock market) would have had to have dropped by 18% to 19%, in order to trigger the same loss that you would experience by moving your money around!

Here's why: When you adjusted your portfolio, you were forced to pay about $3,750 in income tax that you otherwise would not have had to pay. If the stock market had dipped 10%, you would have lost only $2,000 of your investment; if it dropped 20%, you would have lost $4,000. So, you have forced yourself into an unnecessary loss of nearly 19%.

What happens if the stock market drops "only" 10%, and then begins to climb again? You would be worse off by 8%! So the act of shifting your portfolio potentially triggers a larger loss than you would have incurred, had the market dropped fully one-tenth of its value.

What makes a Systematic Withdrawal Plan work so effectively is the tax-deferred growth of the money inside the SWP. And if you are shifting your money around every few years, you are not getting the benefit of the tax deferral — which is critical in an SWP.

If you're looking at investing in a Systematic Withdrawal Plan, I suggest funds such as Templeton Growth, Templeton International Stock, Infinity International, Fidelity International Portfolio, or CI Global — all of them good, solid, long-term funds. (There are a fair number of other funds that qualify in this manner.) You should buy funds like these with the view that the money manager will be the one to move the money around for you; you won't want to do so, because you lack the expertise, and because you don't want to trigger that tax.

Most international fund managers tend to turn the portfolio around every five years or so, which means you would be getting that tax-deferred growth on your money for only that length of time. Infinity, however, follows the Warren Buffett method of investing, and its funds purchase stocks like Walt Disney, Berkshire Hathaway, Coca-Cola, Gillette — Grade A companies that have been around for many decades, and that carry brands recognized in most countries around the globe. These are companies with stocks that have been highly, even stunningly, profitable for many, many years — and Infinity has no intention of selling them. They believe, like the Great Investor Buffett himself, in buying and holding for the very long term. This strategy gives you the best tax deferral of your money — and one of the main things you are looking for in an SWP is as much tax deferral as you can get; that's what makes it work so wondrously.

The Infinity group of funds is one of the most efficient, in terms of tax, and the funds work astonishingly well with the SWP. By the way, if you have $100,000 to invest in an SWP, I suggest you divide it between a couple of funds, just to diversify yourself a little bit. By a couple, I don't mean between eight and ten, but two or three, so you can expose yourself to a few different management styles.

Refer again to the chart on page 88, which is designed to

give you an idea of how dramatic the return differential can be between Periodic Trading and the Buy-and-Hold Strategy.

In this chart, you can compare identical $200,000 investments, both averaging a straight 10% per year compounded rate of return, and being taxed at the 35% marginal tax rate for capital gains. Note how, after thirty years — yes, I know this is a long time — the after-tax return on the Periodic Trading side, which has the tax triggered every five years, is about 4.4%. The buy-and-hold strategy return is 8.5% after tax — a huge difference! After three decades, you would find yourself with $2,338,422 to spend, versus a mere $735,556. Now, which would you rather have?

To my knowledge, only Infinity and AIC mutual funds follow the pure buy-and-hold strategy.

ANOTHER DAY, ANOTHER CHART

Take a look at the chart in the second half of Appendix Seven, which clearly illustrates how an SWP works with a high-quality global fund like Templeton Growth, over different ten-year periods.

Note how it works: Every single line is a complete, separate, and distinct example of what would have happened if you had set up an SWP with the Templeton Growth Fund — investing that $100,000, and taking out $10,000 each year over a decade. What would be left at the end of that period?

As you study the chart, recall that the longer you leave the SWP in place, the greater the chances that the averages will work out to your advantage. Obviously there will be some ten-year periods that are absolutely awful. You should expect this, and be prepared for it. But some ten-year periods will be excellent, of course; never forget that.

What makes this particular chart so valuable is that it truly gauges the risk with this kind of strategy since it covers all of the ten-year periods from 1955 to 1995. Let's take a worst-case scenario, which you can find on the second line down. If your ten-year SWP ran from 1956 to 1966, you began with $100,000, withdrew that full $100,000 over the years, and were still left with $75,400 at the end. I don't think that's too bad. (Try putting $100,000 into a GIC, taking out the full principal over a decade, and still be left with seventy-five grand! Good luck.)

The next worst ten-year period was from 1961 to 1971, when, after taking out $100,000 through systematic withdrawals, you would have had $88,000 left in your account.

And the third worst was the decade running from 1955 to 1965, when you would have been left with $93,492 after ten years of withdrawals.

Isn't it interesting, and informative, that those three "worst" periods were the only ten-year periods of time, out of forty ten-year periods, where you were left with less than you had originally invested?

Let's face it: If you were to invest $100,000 in anything, and over a decade were to withdraw an equal amount, how much would you reasonably expect to be left with at the end of that period? $10,000? $5,000? Zero?

Now that we've looked at the not-too-scary "worst case" scenarios, let's look at some of the best cases. If you ran this classic SWP between 1976 and 1986, depositing $100,000 in the earlier year and withdrawing $10,000 a year over the decade, you would still have $557,325 in your account, ten years later! In other words, in a mere decade, you would have taken all your original money back, and still have over five times your original investment in your account! (Shades of tripping over IBM in its infancy, when its common shares cost only a few dollars!)

You may wish to totally disregard the best-case scenario. Fair enough. But if you do so, you should disregard the worst-case scenario as well. It's clear that, on average, over that forty-year period of time, with a quality mutual fund like Templeton Growth, investors were able to put in $100,000, slowly take out that $100,000 (in a low-taxed fashion), and still be left with more than $100,000 in their accounts. If you are still nervous, why not reduce the withdrawals to the same rate you would receive on a GIC? Who says that you have to take out 10% a year?

How could anyone ask for an investment strategy to do more than that for them? I think the Systematic Withdrawal Plan is one of the best strategies available for anyone. But remember, although these historical examples look very compelling, past performance is no guarantee of future results! To obtain detailed information about any fund, you should read the "simplified prospectus," which contains all the important data you will need.

The Systematic Withdrawal Plan is one of the best means of getting a tax-efficient income from non-RRSP investments, but you have to be comfortable with your portfolio fluctuating if you want use this strategy. If you are not, the strategy described in Chapter Fourteen would be better for you.

CHAPTER ELEVEN

Three Tax Strategies

Think of your finances as a chess board. Each of the investment strategies and each of the classes of assets that you
have are a piece (tool) at your disposal. The purpose of this
book is to show you how you can manipulate the pieces on
your chess board to achieve your desired results — and win.
The first step was to show you how the various component
parts worked. In this chapter, we will have some fun putting
the components together to achieve various results.

The first section, The Plan, is designed for the average
Canadian. The second section, Low-Cost RRSP, is designed
for the high-income, high-spending yuppie who has a problem
saving. The third section is for higher-net-worth, retired, or
near-retired, Canadians.

THE PLAN
Most financial strategies are set up for wealthy investors who
have significant sums of money to invest or large taxable
incomes. This section is not written for those people. It was
created, in fact, for people between the ages of 20 and 45.
Money is usually tight in this period of life, when we have the
largest drain on our income from mortgages, business start-
ups, raising children, insurance, and so much more. Despite

the fact that money is usually short, these are the single most important years to start planning for the future, since there are so many compounding years ahead.

The general rule of thumb is that you should save 10% of your gross income each year if you hope to retire in a manner equal to or better than your current lifestyle. Naturally, the actual outcome at retirement will depend entirely on what you save and how early you begin saving.

The first step is to have a financial plan done, to map out the exact course that you need to take. Generally, your key goals when you are between the ages of 20 and 45 are:

1. To protect your family against the death of any wage earners through life insurance.
2. To protect your family against the disability of any wage earners through disability income protection.
3. To accumulate money in RRSPs.
4. To accumulate money outside of RRSPs.

What is the best way to accomplish your goals?

Let's look at an example to help you picture this better. We will assume that you are a 35-year-old married, male, non-smoker, who is earning $50,000 a year and hopes to retire at age 65. Your wife, 35, works part-time and raises your two children. The family plans to invest $5,000 a year and needs $100,000 worth of life insurance. The balance of the life insurance is through a group plan at work. The maximum RRSP contribution that you can make annually is $4,000, which leaves $1,000 to pay for the insurance and save some money in non-RRSP investments.

How can you do this?

In order to simplify this example, we are going to assume that your family purchases term-to-100 (T-100) insurance, which has a rate that stays the same for life. It has no cash value. (More often, people would purchase "term 10," which increases in cost every ten years. However, this would make the example far more complicated and would not change the outcome dramatically.) It would cost $427 a year for life to purchase $100,000 of term-to-100 insurance.

Look at the second page of Appendix Eight, on the left-hand side of the chart (on the subject of RRSP and Buy Term & Invest the Difference), and you will see an example of this concept. For the purpose of this example, I have assumed an 8% return on investments and that the investment grows completely tax deferred. (As we all know, this is not the case. However, the goal here is to make this example look as good as possible. Another reason for my assumption is that it more than compensates for us using T-100 insurance as discussed above, rather than T-10 insurance. Keep this in mind when you look at the comparisons.)

The alternative to the above course of action is something I call the Registered Family Tax Strategy (RFTS). In essence, the RFTS is very similar to the Family Tax Strategy (FTS) discussed in Chapter Nine; the difference is that a part of it is registered as an RRSP (Registered Universal Life Product). Just think of this as the FTS with an RRSP clinging to the side of it.

As the FTS is designed to facilitate the tax-deferred growth of non-registered money and provide a tax-free income or lump sum withdrawal, all the money left in the plan — including the life insurance — is passed tax free to the named beneficiary (outside of probate) upon the death of the insured.

Let me summarize the RFTS for you. It gives you:

- Tax-deferred savings beyond your annual RRSP contribution limit.
- A choice of different investment options, with excellent growth potential, which may be changed at any time without triggering tax consequences.
- An incentive bonus of 1.25% to 1.75% on top of The Plan's competitive returns.

- The ability to transfer funds from other RRSPs, in order to enhance the incentive bonus feature.
- A means to increase the value of your estate.
- A tax-free retirement income in addition to RRSP income.
- Disability income features, which are included at no additional cost.

If you turn to page 229 of Appendix Eight, you will see a presentation of the RFTS. On the next page is a summary comparison between the RFTS and the more traditional "Buy Term and Invest the Difference Strategy," or the BT&ID.

As you can see, $5,000 is invested into each of these plans for a period of twenty years. By the time you reach the age of 55, the RFTS already has $242,768 in the RRSP, as compared with $197,692 in the BT&ID — a $45,076 advantage. (Both plans have $100,000 worth of insurance.)

The RFTS has $42,283 in the non-RRSP section, as compared with only $28,319 in the BT&ID — a $13,964 advantage. And remember, while money in the RFTS truly grows tax deferred, the BT&ID concept does not, although, in this example, we have given the "Buy Term" way the benefit of assuming that it *does* have this similar attraction.

If you permitted both plans to grow tax deferred until age 69 (with no further investments except the BT&ID's annual $427 insurance cost), the RFTS would *really* start to pull ahead of the other: When you reach 69, the RFTS will have $901,584 in its RRSP/RRIF, compared with $580,659 in the BT&ID, for a very satisfying advantage of $320,925. The non-RRSP investment within the RFTS will have grown to $136,110, compared with only $84,738 in the BT&ID plan — a $51,372 advantage!

Over the last thirty-four years, the total amount invested in The Plan would have been $100,000, compared with $105,978 in the Buy Term and Invest strategy! (Remember that the BT&ID strategy is costing you $427 per year for those fourteen years between ages 55 and 69, so on top of your $100,000 investment, you're paying a total cost of $5,978. In the RFTS plan, on the other hand, the $100,000 worth of term insurance is paid for out of money already in the plan.)

It is easy to see just how powerful and impressive the RFTS is. The question is, *why* is it so superior?

The reasons are identical to the Family Tax Strategy: tax-deferred growth and an incentive bonus of 1.25% to 1.75% on top of The Plan's competitive returns, beginning in year 5.

There may be many readers who look at this and say, "How am I going to afford $5,000 a year in savings?" Remember the deductions-at-source form that we discussed in Chapter Eight, a copy of which is in Appendix Four. If you were at the 40% marginal tax bracket, the $4,000 RRSP contribution would cost you only $200 a month or $2,400 a year as an out-of-pocket expense. The $1,600 a year balance, or about $134 a month, would be provided by Revenue Canada. They would be sending your refund each pay period, as you invested your money in the RRSP. Your true reduction in cash flow would be only $3,400 a year, or about $284 a month.

Both the Family Tax Strategy and the Registered Family Tax Strategy are Universal Life Insurance contracts, issued by NN Life. In this example, the RFTS is a Registered Universal Life contract, while the FTS, described in Chapter Nine, is not registered. All life insurance companies have Universal Life contracts, but before you purchase one, make sure to compare it with at least two others. These are long-term contracts, and you do not want to discover, several years in the future, that you have chosen the wrong company to work with.

Remember, the performance you receive from your investments will always depend on the investment return earned.

THE LOW-COST RRSP STRATEGY:
HIGH INCOME, LOW DISPOSABLE
This plan is especially designed for the yuppie Canadian family who may have good assets and high salaries but whose

cash flow is tight. Between rent or mortgage, the expenses to feed and clothe those children, restaurant bills, expensive clothing, cars, and all the other bills that keep flooding your mailbox every day, you find it difficult to save any money, whether inside or outside an RRSP.

This strategy is designed to permit you to maximize your RRSP and save some money outside the RRSP without any significant loss to your current cash flow or lifestyle.

You accomplish this is by doubling up on tax deductions and using the deductions-at-source form to get you your pro rata refund each pay period rather than waiting until the end of the year. To make this strategy work, you must have a high income and a low debt–service ratio. This ratio is the calculation the banks use to tell them if you can afford the loan payment. They take your gross income and divide it by your yearly payments — interest plus principal. They like to see a number below 35% if possible — that is, no more than 35% of your gross income is being used up by loan payments. The banks do have some flexibility with this percentage, depending on your job security, assets, relationship with the bank, etc.

For the purpose of the example, we will assume that you have a $6,000-a-year RRSP limit, will receive a 10% return on your investments, will pay an 8% interest cost for the loan, and are at a 46% top marginal tax bracket.

Refer to the chart on pages 152–53, which illustrates the results of this strategy.

Here's how the strategy works. You borrow $60,000 to invest. With 8% interest-only payments, you have created a $4,800 annual interest deduction. From the $60,000 investment loan, you set up a Systematic Withdrawal Plan (Chapter Ten) for $6,000 a year. The 10% you make from this investment each year is then used to maximize your $6,000 RRSP contribution. You have now created $10,800 in tax deductions ($4,800 interest plus $6,000 RRSP).

At a marginal tax rate of 46%, you would receive a refund

of $4,968 from Revenue Canada. What did you pay out? You paid out only the $4,800 in interest costs on the loan! You did not pay out the $6,000 you invested in your RRSP — it was taken from the income-flow from your investment loan of $60,000.

If you use the deductions-at-source form to notify Revenue Canada about the $10,800 in deductions that you will have, they will inform your payroll office to remit $4,968 less to them each year. This increases your cash flow by $4,968 ÷ 12, or $414 a month. Use this money to pay your $400-a-month interest cost on the loan for investment purposes.

If you were able to average a return greater than 10% from your loan for investment purposes, you would also have accumulated some money outside the RRSP.

Remember, at some point you will have to pay off the loan for investment purposes.

Are There Any Downsides? Sure, and I've Got To Mention Them

There are always some potential negatives to borrowing to invest, and I've noted them elsewhere in this book. But there are four additional negatives to *this* plan, and it would be negligent and irresponsible for me to leave them out. However, I will give you some ideas about how to overcome them, as well.

Negative Number One: If cash flow is a problem, this idea may not work for you. You need a steady flow of cash to meet the monthly interest payments on the loan. As discussed earlier, this can be overcome with the Deduction at Source Form. However, if you were to lose your job, this form would not help. Make sure you have an emergency cash reserve available in case of such a dilemma. If need be, you could always redeem some of your RRSP, which would be taxable, and use it to pay the interest cost on the loan, which is tax deductible, to buy some time.

THE LOW-COST RRSP STRATEGY

Loan amount	$60,000
Non-registered investment	$60,000
Rate of return	10.00%
Withdrawal rate for RRSP contribution (SWP)	10.00%
Loan rate of interest	8.00%
Marginal income tax rate	46.00%

Year	Non-registered investment	Loan interest (tax deductible)	RRSP contribution (tax deductible)	Total tax deductions	Income tax refund	Accumulated savings (cost)	Projected RRSP
1	60,000	4,800	6,000	10,800	4,968	168	6,600
2	60,000	4,800	6,000	10,800	4,968	336	13,860
3	60,000	4,800	6,000	10,800	4,968	504	21,846
4	60,000	4,800	6,000	10,800	4,968	672	30,631
5	60,000	4,800	6,000	10,800	4,968	840	40,294
6	60,000	4,800	6,000	10,800	4,968	1,008	50,923
7	60,000	4,800	6,000	10,800	4,968	1,176	62,615
8	60,000	4,800	6,000	10,800	4,968	1,344	75,477
9	60,000	4,800	6,000	10,800	4,968	1,512	89,625

Year	Non-registered investment	Loan interest (tax deductible)	RRSP contribution (tax deductible)	Total tax deductions	Income tax refund	Accumulated savings (cost)	Projected RRSP
10	60,000	4,800	6,000	10,800	4,968	1,680	105,187
11	60,000	4,800	6,000	10,800	4,968	1,848	122,306
12	60,000	4,800	6,000	10,800	4,968	2,016	141,136
13	60,000	4,800	6,000	10,800	4,968	2,184	161,850
14	60,000	4,800	6,000	10,800	4,968	2,352	184,635
15	60,000	4,800	6,000	10,800	4,968	2,520	209,698
16	60,000	4,800	6,000	10,800	4,968	2,688	237,268
17	60,000	4,800	6,000	10,800	4,968	2,856	267,595
18	60,000	4,800	6,000	10,800	4,968	3,024	300,955
19	60,000	4,800	6,000	10,800	4,968	3,192	337,650
20	60,000	4,800	6,000	10,800	4,968	3,360	378,015

Figures quoted are projections only and are not guarantees of future performance.

Average withdrawal rate cannot exceed average rate of return without impairment of capital.

Negative Number Two: Let's say that the investment you have chosen for that $60,000 is not bringing in the 10% income you had hoped and planned for. You'd probably been counting on the $6,000 gain from your investment every year to put into your RRSP, as outlined above.

Normally you could withdraw the $6,000 a year via an SWP (Systematic Withdrawal Plan; discussed in Chapter Ten). As long as the $60,000 investment averaged a 10% annual return, this strategy would work. But, depending on how you borrowed the $60,000, there might be a margin feature on the loan. This would cause a problem if the value dropped too much, necessitating the bank to ask for more collateral. (See Chapter Eight for suggested solutions to this problem.)

Negative Number Three: Non-registered (non-RRSP) investments will pay out distributions from time to time that are taxable to varying degrees, depending on whether they are interest, dividends, or capital gains. My spreadsheet did not take these distributions into consideration, as there is no way to know what they might be. Also, when you set up a Systematic Withdrawal Plan (SWP), a portion of the withdrawal is considered refund of capital (tax free) and a portion is taxable capital gains (see the Trimark example in Chapter Ten). This cost has not been accounted for in the spreadsheet either.

If you look back at the spreadsheet for the low-cost RRSP, you'll see that in each year there is a slight surplus when you subtract your out-of-pocket expenses ($4,800 a year interest cost) from the income tax refund ($4,968 a year). The surplus (in this case, $168) will partly compensate for the above costs.

Negative Number Four: You are permitted to deduct the interest costs of a loan for investment purposes. However, as soon as you start taking an income from the investment, the amount you can deduct from your interest expense (in this case $4,800 a year) will be reduced.

A large part of the SWP payment is considered refund of

principal or capital in the initial years. Let's assume that in our low-cost RRSP strategy this amount was $5,000 out of the $6,000 taken out in the first year. This would (according to Revenue Canada) reduce your investment loan to $60,000 – $5,000 = $55,000. The next year, you would be able to deduct only $55,000 x .08% = $4,400 a year for tax-deductible interest expenses. This does not mean that your interest cost has been reduced or that the value of the investment has been reduced; it is simply how your loan is treated for tax purposes.

Clearly this strategy is not designed for everyone. There are too many potential negatives for anyone other than high-income earners who could, if needed, quickly raise sizeable amounts of money.

If you want to retire with dignity, you have to invest for your retirement. There is no way around this fact. Investment strategies like the low-cost RRSP strategy can help you get started with very little effect on your cash flow. However, as time goes on, you will eventually have to devote a percentage of your cash flow to it or any other strategy.

Remember, there is no perfect strategy. The key is understanding the advantages and disadvantages of each in order to incorporate the features that are best for you.

RETIRED LARGE RRSPS

If you are retired or very close to retiring, it is critical that you have a financial plan. The purpose of the plan is not only to confirm that you can continue to enjoy the lifestyle you have become accustomed to, but also to project exactly what your tax and estate situation will look like in the future. If you are fortunate enough to be in a situation where you will clearly not spend all of your savings during retirement, how do you leave your money to the next generation in as tax efficient a manner as possible?

Usually Canadians have money saved inside an RRSP.

Therefore, one of the most frequently asked questions by retired Canadians is when they should start taking money out of their RRSP.

Money inside an RRSP grows tax deferred; however, eventually upon the second spouse's death, all the money that is left in an RRSP/RRIF is brought into the deceased's terminal tax return. The proceeds are fully taxable in that one year. It does not require a large RRSP/RRIF to push that year's tax return into the top marginal tax bracket, potentially resulting in the clawback of all the Old Age Supplement (OAS) paid out to the deceased in that year.

Is it wise to permit an RRSP/RRIF to grow too much, knowing that you will eventually lose about half of it? The only way to know is to look at your financial plan. If it is clear that you will not spend all of your RRSP/RRIF, it makes sense to take more money out of it earlier.

If you do not need the resulting income, you will want to save it outside the RRSP. An equity or stock investment is most tax efficient. The top tax bracket for capital gains is about 35%, depending on the province you live in. The equity investment will also grow tax deferred until you sell it. (There may be some capital gains and dividend distribution, depending on the investment you choose.)

The next question is how to take this income out as tax-efficiently as possible (you do not want to have your OAS clawed back in the process if you are currently receiving it).

The illustration on the next page gives you a pictorial representation of how this strategy would work. The purpose is to move taxable RRSP/RIF money to less-taxable, non-RRSP money. This diagram assumes that we are taking $4,000 a year out of a $50,000 RRSP/RRIF and using it to pay the tax-deductible interest costs on a loan for investment purposes. If that $50,000 investment grew at 9% annually, the resulting $4,500 gain could be left to compound, used as income, invested in an FTS, and so on.

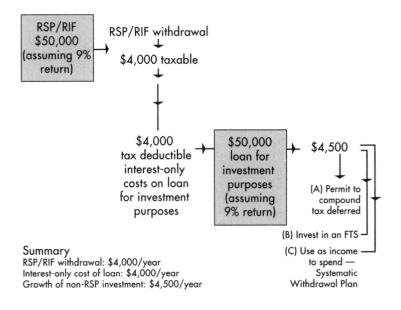

Summary
RSP/RIF withdrawal: $4,000/year
Interest-only cost of loan: $4,000/year
Growth of non-RSP investment: $4,500/year

For the purpose of this example, we are going to assume that we are permitting the $50,000 to compound. (If you want an income from it, refer to the previous section of this chapter to make sure that you are aware of the negatives.) A numerical example of the Retired Large RRSP strategy can be found in the chart on pages 158–59.

In this example, we are assuming that both the RRSP and non-RRSP investments grow at the same rate of 9% a year. (Note that historically, non-Canadian investments have tended to average returns at least 2% to 3% higher than Canadian ones.) The interest rate on the loan for investment purposes is 8%. Each year, 8% is withdrawn from the RRSP to service the loan, and a 46% marginal tax bracket is assumed.

Four thousand dollars is redeemed from the RRSP each year (taxable) and is used to pay the interest costs of the loan for investment purposes (tax deductible). This moves money from the higher-taxed RRSP to the lower-taxed non-RRSP area. After twenty years, we can see that the RRSP would have grown to be worth $75,580, while the non-RRSP would be worth $280,220!

After tax, and after loan repayment, these two would

THE RETIRED LARGE RRSP STRATEGY

Assumed value of RRSP	$50,000
Amount borrowed	$50,000
RRSP withdrawal rate	8%
Loan rate of interest	8%
Investment rate of return	9%
Marginal tax rate	46%
Yearly withdrawal from RRSP (taxable)	$4,000
Yearly loan interest (tax deductible)	$4,000
Yearly tax payable	$0

Year	RRSP value (end of year)	Non-registered value (end of year)
1	50,500	54,500
2	51,045	59,405
3	51,639	64,752
4	52,287	70,579
5	52,992	76,931
6	53,762	83,855
7	54,600	91,402
8	55,514	99,628
9	56,511	108,595
10	57,596	118,368
11	58,780	129,021
12	60,070	140,633
13	61,477	153,290
14	63,010	167,086
15	64,680	182,124
16	66,502	198,515
17	68,487	216,382
18	70,651	235,856
19	73,009	257,083
20	75,580	280,220

Gross value of non-registered investment	280,220
Minus loan repayment	50,000
Taxable capital gain	230,220
Minus tax payable (75% of capital gain x marginal rate)	79,426
Net value of non-registered investment	**150,794**
RRSP value (after tax)	40,813
Plus non-registered investment value	150,794
Total after-tax value using this strategy	**191,607**
After-tax value of RRSP without using this strategy	**151,319**

combine to be worth $191,607. If you had left the $50,000 inside the RRSP, compounded at a 9% return, it would have been worth $151,319 after tax. This strategy has resulted in your net worth increasing by $40,288 after tax!

The strategy works well assuming equal returns both inside and outside the RRSP. In reality, you should expect superior returns outside the RRSP. Would you normally consider borrowing to invest if you could expect only a 1%-per-year better return on your investment, as compared to the interest cost?

Most retired Canadians are proud of the fact that they have no debt. As a result, it is difficult to imagine why a retired Canadian would use this strategy, especially considering the risk associated with a loan. The reason to do it is that after tax you would be about 26% ahead, in terms of portfolio value. However, does that justify the risk?

In Chapter Eight (Borrowing To Invest), we talked about segregated funds as a means of reducing risk when using this strategy. The advantage of segregated funds is that you enjoy a 100% guarantee of principal. This means that if you invest the loan into a segregated fund and leave the money invested for ten years, you are guaranteed not to lose any of your principal. Your only risk now is the interest payments on the loan that is coming from your RRSP.

This strategy is not for everyone; we have discussed the drawbacks of borrowing to invest in Chapter Eight. However, there are many Canadians who are using it successfully. It certainly makes more sense to do this than to leave the money in your RRSP, if you are not going to use it and will ultimately lose half its value in taxes paid to Revenue Canada.

Chapter Twelve

How To Take Money Out of a Corporation

M ore and more Canadians are starting small businesses or creating professional corporations and making a success of them. This is wonderful. But what is resulting from these successes? Usually, a fair amount of money is accumulating *inside* the corporation. And if that money grows to too large an amount, it ends up being taxed at the top marginal tax bracket — a towering 47%. (This rate varies from province to province.)

A lot of clients faced with this situation have asked me, "What can I do? How can I take this money out without being taxed to oblivion?"

One option is to take money out of corporations in dividends; another is to take it out in salary. But both withdrawals are taxable. What help is there for people who have created successful businesses and built up a lot of assets? What should they do with those assets? How can they get some of them out of the company, without being hit brutally with income tax?

There are a number of things you can do.

Strategy 1
One simple solution is to set up a personal loan for investment purposes. The interest costs will be tax deductible on such a

loan. Next, take money out of the corporation, paid to you in the form of salary, which is fully tax deductible by that corporation and taxable to you. Then use that money to pay the tax-deductible interest costs on the loan. By doing this, you end up taking money from the corporation and putting it into your own hands in a fully tax-efficient manner. This in itself does not mean that you have any money to spend. The investment loan has to grow for you to realize a gain with this strategy. We have talked about borrowing to invest in previous chapters, so you know how this strategy works.

Strategy 2

Another strategy is to look at setting up an FTS inside the corporation (see Chapter Nine). Why would you wish to do this? Just as with an individual, the money that the corporation invests in the FTS goes in after tax, so it is not tax deductible. It compounds tax deferred. And the corporation can take tax-free lumps, or a tax-free income out at any time. Upon the death of the insured, the FTS pays out tax free.

When an FTS is owned by a company, the dynamics are very interesting. Normally, when you take money out of a corporation, that money is fully taxable. But when that money is in the form of an insurance policy different regulations come into play. The insured will likely be one of the owners of the business, possibly the oldest owner. Upon the death of the insured, a lump sum is paid from the life insurance policy, which goes into the corporation. The proceeds of the insurance policy can be passed through the corporation to the owners of that firm, through what is called the Capital Dividend Account (CDA), on a tax-free basis.

This strategy is often used to fund buy/sell agreements between partners in a corporation. The tax-free proceeds of the life insurance paid out on the death of the insured are used by the corporation to purchase the deceased partner's shares from his estate. This transfers full ownership of the corporation to the remaining shareholders and gives the estate of the deceased cash. Buy/sell agreements will be discussed in more detail in the next chapter.

You can see why this system can work very well.

Some may look at this strategy and say, "This looks interesting, Brent, but what happens if I need the money?" (A very appropriate question!) An excellent feature of the FTS is that it can be used as collateral for a loan. It is easily cashable (something you don't want to do as cashing out may trigger a lot of tax; using the FTS as collateral is preferable), so the banks and trust companies view it as excellent collateral. They will usually lend to the policy holder on a dollar-loan-per-dollar-cash-value basis, at no more than a prime-plus-one interest rate. This is far superior to loans on inventory, machinery, receivables, or buildings, which do not always receive such good treatment by the banks.

The problem with this strategy is that the life insured does not benefit from the tax-free lump-sum payout.

When a partner retires from a corporation, he usually has no further need of the life insurance policy. If this policy has cash value, the corporation usually lets the retiree take the policy with him. For tax purposes, the cash value would be considered a taxable benefit even though the policy was not redeemed. The retiree can then do with the policy as he pleases.

Strategy 3

There is another strategy that can be used for the corporation to get money out on a tax-free basis. This one "walks the line closely," as they say, so you should probably consult your accountant on this one. Many people across Canada are implementing this strategy, and it works very well, indeed. (Be warned, though — if tens of thousands choose to do it, Ottawa might well step in and disallow it.) Since my purpose is to bring interesting concepts to your attention, how can I resist this one?

Here's how it goes:

Usually investors dislike redemption fees as they limit the investor's flexibility. However, this strategy takes advantage of what would otherwise be viewed as negative — a large redemption fee!

Let's assume the corporation has a lot of cash that is not needed for its operations. There are two partners in the firm, and they want to take money out of the corporation as tax-efficiently as possible. The corporation takes out two Universal Life Insurance policies, with each partner being the insured on a policy. The purpose is to quickly supply capital for a funded buy/sell agreement.

The corporation invests $20,000 a year into each policy. After five years, each policy has an account value of about $120,000; however, each policy has a cash-surrender value of only $35,000. If the policy was held for ten years, the account value and the cash-surrender value would be the same. The difference between the two after five years is the redemption fee, or penalty, for redeeming the plan early (an unusually high redemption fee; however, such fees do exist).

If after five years, the partners decided that the corporation no longer needed the policies, each of them could purchase their policy from the corporation. Revenue Canada views the value of each policy as the cash value. What would it be worth on that day if they were to redeem the policy at fair market value?

Each partner would have to pay the tax that the $35,000 would generate in their hands when added to their other taxable income.

However, if they held the investment for another five years, the redemption fee would be gone. Each of the partners would have taken out an asset worth $120,000 at year five and paid only $17,500 tax each, if they were both at a 50% tax bracket.

Not a bad way to get money out of a corporation with very little tax owed. Once the policy was owned personally, each partner could treat it as a Family Tax Strategy and borrow tax-free lumps or create a tax-free income stream (refer to Chapter Nine for more information).

If you were to take out this insurance policy with the *direct intention* of following this strategy four or five years in the future, it would no doubt fall under GAAR (General Anti-Avoidance Rules); in other words, if you were doing this specifically to avoid tax, it would more than likely be disallowed. But if you just happen to have some money inside your corporation, and you wish to put it into a Universal Life policy to allow it to grow tax deferred, or to quick-fund a buy/sell agreement, this strategy would be considered legal.

CHAPTER THIRTEEN

Free Life Insurance and Funded Buy/Sell Agreements

This chapter's title is a bit of a misnomer. As I've said before, there is very little in life that is truly free. However, as you will soon read, some things come pretty close.

This strategy is designed for anyone who needs life insurance — specifically, the death benefit — and has significant funds outside an RRSP. It also works incredibly well for corporations that have unused cash. What makes this strategy unique is that it is designed to give you back, over a period of more than ten years, all the money that was placed into the plan as a lump sum. After the ten-plus-year period, you will have received a total refund of the money invested, and be left with a paid-up insurance policy.

CORPORATE APPLICATION

An excellent candidate for this strategy would be a business that wants to set up a funded buy/sell agreement. It has a lump sum of money it can use now; however, it feels that it will need it back in the near future, to fund expansion or other corporate needs.

A buy/sell agreement is used when there are two or more partners in the corporation. If one of the partners dies, what happens to that person's shares? Usually, they go to the deceased partner's beneficiaries. But what if those people don't get along with the original partner, or just want to sell their percentage? Where will the original partner get the cash to buy the estate's share of the company?

This is where a funded buy/sell agreement comes in. Each partner has a life insurance contract on his or her own life, and the premiums for these contracts are paid for by the corporation, with the corporation named as the beneficiary and owner. The value of the life insurance should match the value of each partner's share in the company.

If one partner dies, the life insurance pays out tax free to the corporation. This lump sum is used by the remaining partner(s) to purchase the shares from the deceased partner's estate. This ensures that any remaining partners are not burdened with a heavy debt (which would be incurred in buying out the estate) or forced to work with the beneficiaries, who may not be agreeable. In buy/sell agreements, the sale on death is usually compulsory.

Many corporations use term insurance as their insurance vehicle for the buy/sell agreement. I do not recommend this, though, for the following reasons:

1. The cost of term insurance keeps increasing over the years, making this alternative more expensive in the long run.
2. As the corporation grows in value, the partners will need to add to their insurance. What happens if one of the partners becomes uninsurable?
3. Corporations can have very unprofitable years. If money is exceptionally tight in any given year, partners will tend to cancel the life insurance that's being used to fund the buy/sell agreement. This can lead to short-term gain, long-term pain.
4. If the corporation is thirty days late in paying a term insurance premium, the life insurance company can cancel the policy.

5. Most term insurance contracts expire when the beneficiary turns 70 or 80. What happens if the company is still in existence? How will the estate problem be handled?

NON-CORPORATE APPLICATION

This plan should not be confused with the Family Tax Strategy, or FTS, which I have discussed earlier. The FTS is designed for investors who are looking for tax-free compounding for their non-RRSP money. The lump sum invested and the income that can ultimately be derived from the FTS should not be drawn upon for at least ten years. Therefore, the FTS is for people who are looking for tax-free compounding of their non-needed, non-RRSP money. Insurance is not the primary reason to purchase an FTS. It is, rather, a pleasant by-product.

The strategy being described in this chapter is designed for investors who need the insurance and want to get back the money they used to pay for it — and as quickly as possible.

How does it work? I believe the best product for this strategy is the Intrepid II Universal Life product, which is marketed by Maritime Life. They call this strategy the "Leveraged Premium Program." You will find a complete breakdown of this insurance program, which I am using in the following example, in Appendix Nine.

I have assumed that a family, as opposed to a corporation, is undertaking this strategy; however, it works the same way for individuals and corporations. John and Mary are both 50 and both are non-smokers. They want the insurance for estate purposes, so the insurance will not be needed until the last spouse dies. The insurance they choose is called the Joint Last-To-Die. They have decided to invest $100,000 as a lump sum and want the money refunded to them over a twelve-year period beginning in year 1. If we look at the spreadsheet that starts on page 234 in Appendix Nine, the fourth column from the left represents the money going back to the owners, John and Mary. In year 1, it starts at $10,766; in year 2, it is

$10,983, until the last portion of the $100,000 is refunded in year 12 ($3,120). The Universal Life policy (FTS) is used as collateral to give John and Mary their $100,000 loan. The initial value of the death benefit purchased is $690,802. The value of the death benefit increases over time. This can be seen in the second column from the right (net amount to estate). The gross amount to estate, third column from the right, represents the death benefit before the loan is paid back.

After twelve years, their $100,000 has been paid back, and if the interest rate on the loan and the investment return average 8%, they should still have $55,081 net cash value left in the policy.

As is the case for the FTS, the Universal Life Insurance policy does not permit all of the money to be tax sheltered in the plan from day one. The money is placed into a deposit account, which transfers money automatically every year into the Intrepid II Universal Life contract for seven years. There will, therefore, be some tax payable passed on to John and Mary each year, until all the money is in the plan. They will not receive a cheque, simply a form for their taxes saying that they have earned $X of interest income or capital gain.

The investment mix John and Mary choose within the plan will determine how quickly they can take money out. The larger the percentage in guaranteed interest investments, such as GICs, the more they can take out. John and Mary decide to invest all of their money in equities. Depending on your own requirements, you can custom-design the scenario to fit your needs. This program could have been structured, for example, to permit over $50,000 to have been taken out in year 1, if it was needed; however, the investment would have to have gone into GICs.

The way this investment mix was set up, the maximum loan to Cash Saving Value (CSV) is 75%. (This loan can go as high as 95%.) Therefore, in year 20, there is a CSV of $355,857, and an accumulated loan of $187,995. If John and Mary needed extra money, they could borrow up to 75% of the $355,995, or $266,996. There is already an outstanding loan of $187,995, which means that $79,001 is still available, should the need arise.

Remember: This contract is not guaranteed. It assumes an 8% return on investments. Your actual situation will depend on your investment return. I like to use an 8% rate of return. But the S&P 500 has averaged more than 15% over the last ten years and is one of the investment choices.

As you will appreciate, this is a reasonably complicated strategy. Be sure to consult with a knowledgeable insurance agent, and read all of the fine print and disclosures that Maritime, or whatever company you are dealing with, provides.

This plan allows you to pay for insurance, get all the money refunded over time, and still have the coverage. Hence, you could say it is free. Naturally, you *do* have to have the money in the first place!

Chapter Fourteen

A Guaranteed Income, with No Risk!

The strategy I'm going to describe in this chapter is designed for investors who wish to have a guaranteed flow of income but want absolutely no risk of losing their investment. It is far more tax efficient than merely living off the interest on your GICs or term deposits. This is designed for non-registered money. In other words, it does not work for money within an RRSP. It is usually used only by retirees.

This strategy was created by the insurance industry years ago and is called a Back-to-Back. It involves purchasing an annuity and a life insurance policy. These two products combined will give you a higher after-tax income than living off the interest from your non-registered GICs. Before we look at an example, let me explain the strategy in more detail.

An annuity is a product sold by a life insurance company. You agree to give your money to that insurance company, and they guarantee to give you fixed payments by the month, by the year, by the quarter, or semi-annually for the rest of your life.

These payments are made up of both interest and principal (as are SWPs — see Chapter Ten). Upon death, the income payments stop and there is no estate value left. Therefore, a life insurance policy is purchased for the same amount of money that is placed into the annuity. The life insurance policy returns your initial investment back to the estate tax free.

In a way, annuities are like a mortgage. When you take out a mortgage on a house, you have to make payments that are based on the interest rate, the amount you are borrowing, and the period over which it will be paid back. What happens with annuities is the reverse: You are giving the money to an insurance company, which uses actuarial tables on the expected life span of the average person to project, based on current interest rates, what they will pay out to you monthly for the rest of your life.

In Appendix Ten, you will find an example for a retired couple both aged 65 and both non-smokers. The income is to continue until the second spouse dies. A joint second-to-die life insurance policy and second-to-die annuity is purchased to facilitate this. The annual annuity payment is $6,962.02, of which $2,462.47 is taxable as interest income. The balance is considered refund of the $100,000 initial investment and is tax free. I have assumed a 46% tax bracket necessitating $1,132.74 taxes payable each year.

A joint second-to-die Term-100 insurance policy would cost $1,482 a year. The after-tax and insurance cost income generated from the annuity is $4,347.28 a year. This is what is left to spend. It would be equivalent to a pre-tax return of 7.93%.

I have assumed a 5% return for the GIC. But if you look at the example in the appendix closely, you will notice that the annual interest from the GIC is $5,074.10, not $5,000. This is not a mistake. The insurance premium has to be paid in advance and the GIC does not pay its interest until the end of the year. To compensate, $101,482 has been invested into the GIC (an extra $1,482, the cost of the life insurance premium for one year).

The $5,074.10 is before-tax interest. Assuming a 46% tax rate, $2,334.09 would have to be paid in tax. This would leave $2,740.01 to spend. The Back-to-Back strategy provides $1,607.27 a year more to spend after tax than the straight GIC.

Any time you are dealing with investments that are fully guaranteed, the income produced is usually interest income. With this type of investment vehicle, the question of money lost from inflation is simply not an issue. Purchasing power is lost to inflation over time.

Generally speaking, I would not recommend that you put all your money into the Back-to-Back concept. Rather, I would urge that you have at least part of your money in an SWP (Systematic Withdrawal Plan), usually in combination with a Back-to-Back.

The best time to purchase a Back-to-Back is when prevailing interest rates are high, because you don't want to lock in low interest rates for the rest of your life, and these interest rates can have a significant impact on the income you will eventually receive.

You also have to be insurable, of course. If you are seriously considering setting up a plan like this, always make sure — and I can't stress this enough — that you qualify for the life insurance first, before you purchase the annuity. I am sad to report that every year, I hear about several men or women who do this in the wrong order.

One other thing: For safety purposes, you should purchase the annuity from a different company than you buy the insurance from, a sensible strategy that most advisors will suggest. First, apply for the insurance — without giving them any money. Merely tell them that you will pay for the premium when the insurance is approved. Once the insurance has been approved, you will have about thirty days to accept it. Then, and only then, do you purchase the annuity.

Set the life insurance so that you pay the premiums monthly; the annuity will pay you an income monthly. You end up with a high, 100% guaranteed income that is tax preferred. As you can see in the Back-to-Back examples in this book, you will end up *significantly* better off than if your money were simply invested in a straight GIC.

Chapter Fifteen

Saving for a Child's Education

M ost families lack a solid plan for how to pay for the post-secondary education of their children. Only a very small percentage put money aside in any formal way. Of those who do, many use savings accounts or Canada Savings Bonds, or simply plan on taking funds from their investments when the money is needed. One farm family interviewed recently declared that their plan was based on selling one of their tractors when it was time for their children to go to university!

Let's take a closer look at the various methods of saving for a child's education.

One traditional method was to have a savings account in a bank, which would be used later for educational purposes. If grandparents gave, say, $500 towards their grandchildren's education, it went into a savings account, where it would be safe.

It is estimated that there are hundreds of millions of dollars in savings accounts across Canada waiting for children to use the money for post-secondary schooling. The problem with these accounts is clear: Interest rates are usually around 1%, which is not going to allow for very much growth of the money — especially when inflation averages 1% to 2% per year, and has been five times that (or even more) over the past few decades.

GICs and term deposits are a better way to earn money on savings for a child's education, but there are several problems with them as well. A minimum deposit is usually required, and it must be locked in for a specified period of time. While these are undeniably secure as far as the growth of the money goes, you pay substantial penalties if you have a family emergency and need to liquidate the money on short notice.

Canada Savings Bonds have long been one of the favoured savings plans of parents and grandparents for educating subsequent generations. During the war years of 1914–1918 and 1939–1945, Canadians put money into CSBs with pride, assured that their investments were secure. The government backed them, and purchasers could always get their money out, even on a day's notice, if they needed it. Security, along with reasonable interest rates — especially compared with savings accounts in banks — made them attractive.

THE RESP

Before 1998, I never recommended registered educational savings plans — the famous RESPs — because they didn't make a lot of sense to me. However, there were some changes in the tax laws that year that suddenly made them more attractive. Today, RESPs warrant serious consideration. (As you can see, things can change quickly in the world of financial planning.)

What was the cause of this turn-around in my own thinking, and the suggestions I made to my clients?

An RESP originally worked like this: You put after-tax money into a registered plan. Inside the plan, it grew tax deferred. But when you took the money out in the future, it was taxable. This did not seem very attractive to me! There was no tax deduction and the money was taxable in the future. And if the child was not academically inclined, you lost all the gains on that invested money and received only the principal back! I used to recommend in-trust accounts to parents who wanted to save money for their children's education.

Then came those important, very attractive changes to our tax laws in 1998. You can now save up to $4,000 per beneficiary per calendar year, for twenty-one years, to a maximum of $42,000 per beneficiary in the plan. You must collapse the plan within twenty-five years of the start date. And not only that — the educational institutions that are acceptable now range from universities to community colleges and much more.

Just like an RRSP, there is a penalty of 1% per month on amounts contributed over the yearly allowable limit, until the over-investment is withdrawn or until the next calendar year. During that year, your contribution limit of $4,000 will be reduced by the previous year's over-contribution.

Here is the truly beautiful part: With the new RESP, the federal government in Ottawa adds 20% per year onto the first $2,000 of RESP contribution for each child up to the age of 18. Contributors with children who were 16 or 17 would receive this grant only if they had made RESP contributions of at least $100 per year for the previous four years, or if the previous contribution total was at least $2,000.

Once you have set up an RESP, you can carry forward any unused room to future years. However, you can apply for only a maximum of $800 in grants in a single year per beneficiary.

Remember, you have to apply for the grant. This requires a separate form from the standard RESP application form. Furthermore, you must apply for the grant every year that you make a contribution to the RESP. The grant is paid directly into the RESP, and you need a Social Insurance Number to receive this grant.

Once I had looked at these new rules closely, I began to tell my clients, "Yes, you are permitted to put in up to $4,000 a year, but I recommend that you put in $2,000 at first, because you get that government grant of 20% only up to $2,000. This makes good sense. Since you don't get any grant beyond the two grand, putting more in right off the bat doesn't give you any additional advantage."

Clearly, putting $2,000 into an account, to receive that additional $400 from the government, makes sense. But what happens if your son or daughter chooses *not* to attend a post-secondary school?

You can always withdraw the contributions from the RESP tax free. However, if withdrawals of capital are made before the beneficiary begins a post-secondary education, the Canadian Educational Savings Grant, equal to 20% of the capital withdrawn, must be repaid. In other words, for each dollar taken out of the RESP, twenty cents — representing the grant you received — must be repaid. You do not repay any of the growth that the grant made.

If you are a Canadian resident and have had the RESP for ten years, and none of your beneficiaries plan to attend a post-secondary institution by the age of 21, the growth of the money invested in the RESP can be taken out as accumulated income payments. However, the growth will be taxed at your marginal rate, and there will be an additional 20% income-tax penalty on top. (Some plans have an up-front cost of $2,000, which would be lost as well.)

If you have the contribution room in your RRSP or in a spousal RRSP, you are permitted to roll over the growth in the RESP, up to a maximum of $50,000. No tax is triggered when you do this. However, you have to have the contribution room, so if it looks like your child or children will not be attending a post-secondary institution, start saving your contribution room as the beneficiary approaches 21. Also, keep in mind that when you roll this money into an RRSP, you will not receive a tax deduction for the amount.

In summary, if your beneficiary does not attend a post-secondary institution, you can withdraw tax free all the contributions you made into the RESP. The growth can then either be rolled into the contributor's RRSP or spousal RRSP, or be cashed in. If you choose to cash it in, the proceeds are taxable, as discussed earlier. However, when the accumulated income payment is made, the RESP must be closed by the end of February of the year following that of the first payment.

Another new benefit is that the subscriber can use the money to further his or her own education! The RESP can be used to cover the expenses of attending most post-secondary institutions across Canada, and many that are outside the country, as well. Generally, the programs must run at least three consecutive weeks (thirteen weeks, for those outside Canada), with at least ten hours of courses per week. Some correspondence courses also qualify.

I've heard of one application whereby adults may choose to (say) take a three-month course on The Ruins of Italy or The Architecture of Ancient Greece; there are many such courses that qualify for university credit or credit from any acknowledged institution. So if your children choose to not continue their higher education, you or even your parents (your children's grandparents, that is) can use that money to cover the tuition, room and board, books, and other educational expenses of such studies overseas!

The subscriber (parent or grandparent) has the power to tell the plan administration when and how much to pay the beneficiary (child or children). However, once you start taking the growth out, it must be fully withdrawn by the end of February of the year following that of the first payment.

As you can see, the RESP has become far more flexible than ever before, and the chance of someone in the family using that money is now improved, as compared with any time in the past. And don't forget that nice little $400 "gift" from the government!

MUTUAL FUNDS IN TRUST FOR A CHILD

Another popular investment in past years has been mutual funds in trust for children or grandchildren. A number of things need to be in place for a proper trust account to exist and to work. (Most in-trust accounts don't have these features; they are not proper trusts, according to law.)

On the next page you will find a little letter to use with an in-trust account. It contains the three components necessary to make it a legal trust: the settler/donor, the trustee, and the beneficiary. Keep a copy of this completed document and make sure your financial advisor keeps a copy. This letter will save you the legal fees and accounting fees usually incurred in setting up an in-trust account — generally around $2,000 to set the trust up, as well as annual fees to administer the account.

The first person — for example, parent, grandparent, or family friend — to establish the account and put money into the plan is considered to be the settler or donor. Anyone else can put money into the plan thereafter.

The next party, the trustee, is given full discretionary powers on the account, and technically, he or she has the fiduciary role. In other words, legally, he or she is considered the parent or guardian, who makes sure that the money is managed in the best interests of the child. The settler/donor and the trustee cannot be the same person. If the grandparent is the settler/donor, the parents could be the trustee. Or one parent could be the settler/donor and the other parent could be the trustee. The only note of caution is to remember that, in the event of a divorce, the trustee maintains power over the account.

In addition, you should ponder the implications of a recent case with Revenue Canada. It was found that if the depositing parent (the settler) is related by marriage to the trustee of the account, the "informed trust" is controlled by the parents and is subject to taxation. Where possible, it is best to have a grandparent as settler/donor.

The last component is the beneficiary, who is, of course, the child.

By listing the name of the settler/donor, the trustee, and the

LETTER TO SET UP AN IN-TRUST ACCOUNT

Brent Bullis and Associates
10104 – 103rd Avenue, Suite 2300
Edmonton, Alberta T5J 0H8

Re: Account # _____

Dear Brent,

The intention of this trust account is for accumulation of funds for the eventual benefit of _____. In this regard, please be advised of the following:

- *The Settler/Donor.* This trust account is being established by _____ who will be contributing cash or investments from time to time to the trust.
- *The Trustee.* _____ is given a full discretion as to the investment of the trust property.
- *The Beneficiary.* The investments are for _____ who will ultimately receive the assets in the trust and will benefit from any growth or suffer any loss in the investments.
- This Trust Agreement is irrevocable.

Yours truly,

_____   _____
Signed   Date

beneficiary, and having the settler/donor and the trustee sign, you will have legally set up a proper trust. Now, generally speaking, the trust should not be touched until the child turns 18. However, this trust has been set up for the benefit of the child or children, and it can be used for anything that will benefit the child. The RESP or in-trust account can have multiple beneficiaries.

Additional problems with the informal trust include the following: Upon reaching the age of 18, the beneficiary is legally entitled to take control of the money. It makes no difference whether the parents feel the child is mature enough to handle the money or not. Informal trusts are not creditor-proof, either. If the parent gets into financial difficulties, these accounts can be seized by creditors, and all the sacrificing on behalf of the child can be lost. A formal trust takes care of the above problems; however, the cost of setting one up is prohibitive for most Canadians.

Between the two concepts discussed above — the RESP and the in-trust account — I would recommend that the first $2,000 go into the RESP, because of that generous 20% grant from Ottawa. It's free money, and everyone should take advantage of it. For any additional amounts you are looking at saving, the in-trust account should be of great interest, because it can go into any fund you choose. The money compounds tax deferred (if it is invested in equities), and when it comes time for higher education, the money is passed to the child. The capital gains tax is triggered in the hands of the child, not in those of the parent.

Some parents decide that they will simply "put money aside" in their own name and pay for the education of their children out of that money. The problem with this strategy is that they end up paying tax on all gains over the entire period. They would have been better off setting up an in-trust account earlier.

Many parents, as they review the new RESP rules, ask, "I currently have money in an in-trust account, because I didn't like the way RESPs were originally run before this grant started being offered, back in 1998. May I take money out of my in-trust account, and put it into an RESP, in order to get that 20% grant?"

Generally speaking, the answer is no. However, there is a solution to this problem: Make the minor child both the beneficiary of *and* the contributor to the RESP. With this procedure, children can use their own money (the in-trust account) to invest in an RESP. The next question is, what if the children do not pursue a post-secondary education with this set-up? They must repay the federal grant, and then redeem the original contribution (tax free) and transfer the accumulated income to an RRSP in their first years of employment.

If contributors/beneficiaries do not continue with their post-secondary education and cannot find a job that will allow RRSP deduction room, they can transfer $2,000 to an RRSP as an over-contribution, cash out the remaining accumulated income, then pay the extra 20% tax on top of their marginal tax rate. Most likely, their taxable income will be low, so their tax rate will be lower than the rate their parents would have incurred as contributors.

The only real drawback to this strategy is that because the donor/settler is a minor, the RESP can be invested only in GICs, as a minor may not own securities.

POOLED RESPs

A third type of investment, which many readers will remember, are the pooled RESPs.

Before 1998, these were savings plans set up as charitable donations or non-profit companies. Salespeople approached parents and encouraged them to put money into these plans, but if their children did not choose to pursue a post-secondary education, they lost the gains on the investments and got back only the principal. If the plan covered several children and some of them continued their education and some didn't, the gains would be divided among the number who chose to go to college or university. In other words, "the last people standing" would get the money and the real rewards. Over the past few years, more and more young people have been going on to study at post-secondary institutions, so the individual payouts to the beneficiaries have become significantly lower than they used to be.

The advantage of an individual RESP is clear: You control the money. It is yours — as opposed to being in a pool, where ultimately you don't know how much money you are going to receive when your child eventually chooses higher education. Furthermore, these pooled scholarship plans are set up in a way that forces the administrators to save in 100% guaranteed investments. This is certainly attractive and "safe," but if you set up an in-trust account, you can invest in equities, which usually means that the return will be a little higher than the pooled RESPs.

A RECENT SURVEY OF INTEREST

As I was writing this chapter, the YTV television network announced a national survey taken in the summer of 1998. The survey concentrated on "tweens," which is a catch-all term for youngsters between the ages of 9 and 14. Here is what it came up with:

- Seventy-nine percent of these tweens said that they wanted to go to college or university, up from 67% a year earlier.

- The largest percentage of tweens who responded favourably to the statement "I plan to go to college or university some day" was found in Atlantic Canada (87%) and British Columbia (81%).

- The lowest percentage who agreed with that statement was in the Prairies (72%), followed by Ontario (77%), but in both cases, we were still seeing well over two out of three youth reacting favourably to higher education in their future.

- Tweens from higher-income families were more likely to want to attend post-secondary institutions.

- More than nine out of ten tweens (91%, to be exact) who came from families with incomes of over $75,000 a year planned to study beyond high school.

- Even in lower-income brackets, the numbers were in the 75% range.

The survey, conducted by Creative Research International, came to a fairly obvious conclusion: Education is extremely important to pre-adolescents and adolescents. And you may be pleased to hear that fully three-quarters of these youngsters felt that "having good marks in school" was the epitome of "cool," and 98% agreed with the statement that "education is important to my future."

The researchers concluded, "The generation between the ages of 9 and 14 are sold on higher education. If you have a teen at home, you might want to start socking away some major money."

HEAD START EDUCATION INSURANCE PLANS

A new option has recently become available. It's called Head Start Education Insurance Plans Inc. This is a relative newcomer in the field of education savings plans, but the product it offers responds to most of the problems found in traditional savings methods, mutual funds, and RESPs. This product is designed to fit into the budget of any parent, is under the control of both parents (until they choose to turn it over to the child), can be used for anything else dreamed of (if the child does not go to a post-secondary institution), and is not under direct control of the government for choice of investments!

The product is tax-advantaged and creditor-proof and includes some features that no other plan on the market contains. For example, it has a life insurance component that stays with the child for life, once approved health requirements for the plan have been met. Future health problems do not affect the plan. The money can be accessed at any time after the first six years of the plan in the event of the student needing a tutor to improve grades for university entrance requirements. If the child does not go to university, but a sibling wants to, the parents can — with no penalty or decision deadline — use the money for the sibling.

There are no formal trusts to be set up, and investment deposits are guaranteed by CompCorp in the same way that your savings accounts at the bank are insured, up to

$60,000. The fund does not collapse after university, but can be continued as a retirement plan for the child, or if the parents wish, it can be transferred to their RRSP fund if it is not used for an education.

Additional deposits can be made with minimal paperwork when the grandparents send the child a gift towards their education, and parents have control over where the money is invested. This allows them to choose funds with higher returns, or guaranteed funds. The government does not regulate the choice of segregated funds.

This product is truly remarkable, as you can see. It gives both the discipline that most parents want for their children's education savings fund, along with low management fees, which are set at $42 a year regardless of the amount invested, and the flexibility to use the funds for what is truly in the best interests of the child.

At the time of writing, Head Start Education Insurance Plans Inc. was doing business only in the province of Alberta. However, there are some interesting insurance products available generally that you may want to investigate. NN Life has a particularly good one.

Here are ten questions that all Canadians should ask themselves — and an advisor — before purchasing an educational savings plan for a child or grandchild:

1. As a parent, how long will I have control of the fund?
2. Does the government restrict the choice of funds I can invest in?
3. Is the plan safe from creditors in the event of family financial problems?
4. If my child does not go to university or college, is there a loss of any of the initial investment or growth on the fund?
5. Can I have access to the money prior to my child's enrolment in a post-secondary institution, if it is needed?

6. What will my rate of return be, and do I have any control over it?
7. Is the fund invested with a solid company?
8. What are the tax implications of the fund?
9. Will the fund grow at a faster rate than inflation?
10. Does the plan collapse at a certain date?

Understanding the Risk/Reward Tradeoff

D o you have realistic expectations about both the upside *and* the downside of your portfolio performance?

In September 1997, Marketing Solutions Inc. — Canada's leading research and business development consulting firm for individual producers and investment firms — conducted a survey of Canadians on their understanding of stock market risk. One of the questions was: "In your opinion, over the next ten years, what is the greatest percentage drop we are likely to see in the Canadian stock market in any one year?"

Eighteen percent of the people surveyed said they could not answer the question. Of those who did answer, 11% thought the greatest percentage drop would be more than 20%, another 40% thought it would be between 10% and 20%, and nearly half (49%) believed it would be less than 10%.

How would you answer this question? Would you be part of the small group who correctly answered "more than 20%"?

By helping you understand what history has shown us about the relationship between risk and reward, I hope to better prepare you for what lies ahead. (Thanks to Dan Richards, President of Marketing Solutions, Ibbotson Associates and the

Wall Street Journal for permitting me to reproduce some of their findings.)

Every investor needs to understand four basic points:

1. Over the long term, stocks have dramatically outperformed all other investment alternatives.
2. The price you pay for long-term performance is short- to mid-term volatility.
3. You can't avoid short-term losses if you want to enjoy long-term returns.
4. In the course of a long time span, short- to mid-term volatility is irrelevant.

The key point to recognize is that you are trading off risk and return. Let's look at various portfolios to see what you would have had to endure over a fifty-three-year period to achieve their long-term compounded per annum return. (These numbers are based on the U.S. market.)

Trading Off Risk Versus Return
53 Years from 1945 to 1997

Ratio stocks/bonds (%)	Number of years with losses greater than				Worst loss (%)	Average return (%)
	5%	10%	15%	20%		
100/0	8	4	1	1	(26.5%)	12.9%
60/0	3	1	—	—	(14.3%)	10.3%
40/60	1	—	—	—	(7.9%)	8.8%
0/100	1	—	—	—	(6.1%)	5.8%

Now look at the next chart, which shows long-term return by asset class for Canada from 1950–1998. It also shows the cost of living (the rate of growth needed to preserve your standard of living) also known as the inflation rate. The Real Return heading demonstrates how much more or less you would have at your disposal each year, assuming you were at a 40% marginal tax rate and were permitting your money to preserve its purchasing power (permitting the lump sum to grow 4.2% per year) on average over a forty-eight-year period.

Long-Term Returns by Asset Class (1950–1998)		Real Returns	
Cost of living	4.2%		
Ninety-day T-bills	6.4%	T-bill	-0.36
Long-term bonds	7.6%	Bal	0.36
Five-year GICs	7.8%	CIC	0.48
Canadian stocks	11.2%	CAN	3.56
U.S. stocks	13.9%	U.S.	5.53

Note how five-year GICs actually outperformed bonds by 0.2% per year over this period. The chart also confirms what most of us already know: The U.S. market has outperformed the Canadian market.

Analysis of the chart leads to a shocking conclusion: If you had invested outside the RRSP in a T-Bill, your purchasing power would have declined yearly by 0.36%. If you had invested in bonds or GICs, the real return on your investment would have been only 0.36% and 0.48% per year, respectively. In other words, if you had invested $100,000 in bonds, and wanted your investment to preserve its purchasing power after tax, you would have had only $360.00 to spend each year. On the other hand, the real return on Canadian and U.S. stocks — after tax on the capital gain is triggered each year — yields 3.56% and 5.53%, respectively. If you had invested $100,000 in U.S. stocks, you would have had $5,530 to spend annually.

Here's an example to help clarify the numbers. Let's assume you are 40 years old, self-employed, and plan to retire at 65. If you saved $10,000 a year and invested in the previously discussed portfolios within your RRSP, the results twenty-five years from now would look like this:

	Average Return	Value After 25 Years
100% Stocks	12.9%	$1,729,890.06
60% Stocks/40% Bonds	10.3%	$1,134,925.50
40% Stocks/60% Bonds	8.8%	$894,646.90
100% Bonds	5.8%	$564,377.71

You can see that a relatively small increase in investment return per year can make a significant difference in the value of your portfolio over time.

The question is: What rate of return does your portfolio need to achieve to enable you to retire in the lifestyle you desire? Once you have completed your financial plan and determined the compounded per annum return, the next step is to set up your portfolio. Since nothing in life is free, there is a risk involved in any decision you make. But you need to determine if the risk is short or long term.

The statistics you have already seen demonstrate the long-term risk, but what is the short-term risk?

If you had invested your money in any one-year period over the seventy-two year period between 1924 and 1996, and had invested 100% in Canadian stocks, you would have lost money 26% of the time. Over a three-year period, you would have lost money 17% of the time; over five years, 10%; over ten years, only 2%; and if you had invested in any fifteen-year period (or more) you would not have lost any money whatsoever (source: William M. Mercer).

You can see that the longer your money remains invested, the greater the probability that you will make money. However, it is a bit disconcerting to discover that if you had invested in 100% Canadian stocks for only a one-year period you would have lost money more than a quarter of the time.

Human nature being what it is, you might be tempted to try to time the market to avoid — or try to avoid — drops in the market. But take a look at what would have happened if you had missed ten, twenty, thirty, and forty of the best trading days, assuming a $1,000 lump-sum investment from October 1988 to September 1997:

THE IMPACT OF "CALLING" THE MARKET
10 Years from October 1988 to September 1997

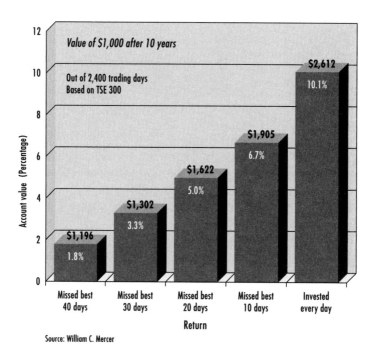

Source: William C. Mercer

If you are going to try to time the market, make sure you get it right. Otherwise the results can be devastating. The question is: Can you afford to time the market?

Templeton Management has a very interesting example that illustrates the difference between investing $5000 a year for twenty-five years (into the Templeton Growth Fund) on the day the stock market was the highest (the worst) versus investing on the day the stock market was at its lowest (the best). In each case, you would have invested $125,000.

THE "BEST" TIME TO INVEST

The left half of the chart below outlines the results of having invested $5,000 for each of the twenty-five years on the day the market reached its peak stock prices. The right half shows the results of having invested on the lowest day for stock prices in each of the twenty-five years.

Date of Market High*	Cumulative Investment	Value of Account on December 31	Date of Market Low*	Cumulative Investment	Value of Account on December 31
01/11/73	$ 5,000	$ 4,474	12/03/73	$ 5,000	$ 4,873
03/13/74	10,000	8,043	12/06/74	10,000	9,370
07/15/75	15,000	16,212	01/02/75	15,000	20,240
09/21/76	20,000	29,237	01/02/76	20,000	36,457
01/03/77	25,000	44,908	11/02/77	25,000	50,836
09/08/78	30,000	62,657	02/28/78	30,000	72,122
10/05/79	35,000	83,014	11/07/79	35,000	95,432
11/20/80	40,000	111,989	04/21/80	40,000	130,064
04/27/81	45,000	115,576	09/25/81	45,000	134,260
12/27/82	50,000	137,961	08/12/82	50,000	101,160
11/29/83	55,000	190,571	01/03/83	55,000	223,548
01/06/84	60,000	212,401	07/24/84	60,000	248,600
12/16/85	65,000	292,364	01/04/85	65,000	343,141
12/02/86	70,000	355,114	01/22/86	70,000	417,092
08/25/87	75,000	340,930	10/19/87	75,000	400,564
10/21/88	80,000	387,938	01/20/88	80,000	455,681
10/09/89	85,000	474,748	01/03/89	85,000	447,965
07/16/90	90,000	414,470	10/11/90	90,000	487,528
12/31/91	95,000	545,279	01/09/91	95,000	635,514
06/01/92	100,000	632,932	10/09/92	100,000	737,163
12/29/93	105,000	867,599	01/20/93	105,000	1,011,311
01/31/94	110,000	905,510	04/04/94	110,000	1,054,860
12/13/95	115,000	1,038,643	01/30/95	115,000	1,162,601
12/27/96	120,000	1,234,824	10/01/96	120,000	1,437,899
08/07/97	125,000	1,450,625	04/14/97	125,000	1,689,151

Average Annual Rate of Return 16.02%   Average Annual Rate of Return 17.81%

* The market is represented by the Dow Jones Industrial Average of 30 stocks.

If you had invested $5000 a year on the day that the stock market was the lowest, your investment would have grown to $1,689,151 (an average annual return of 17.81%). Alternatively, if you had invested each year on the day the highest stock market price was attained, your investment would have grown to $1,450,625 (an annual return of 16.02%).

Clearly, dollar-cost averaging reduces the risk in investing. I suggest that the risk of trying to time the stock market is too great. Invest regularly and invest for the long term — it's the only way you can be sure to achieve your goals.

Are your expectations realistic? Now that you have read this book, I hope you see the importance of having a financial plan and understand that an investment is only a tool — a means to an end, not an end in itself. Remember:

1. Purchase investments that reflect the needs outlined in your financial plan.
2. Set realistic expectations for yourself, looking at both the upside and the downside of any investment plan.
3. Look at all of your investments on an after-tax, after-inflation basis.
4. Review your plan regularly to make sure you are on track.
5. Allow compounding and time to work for you, not against you.

Finally, I would like to suggest that you type out the following two paragraphs, and place them on the front of your investment binder or portfolio to guide you through stock market fluctuations. Before you make any adjustments to your portfolio, reread these paragraphs:

I understand that the stock market is inherently volatile. Based on long-term historical performance, I can expect to lose money in stocks an average of one in every four years.

I am willing to put up with these inevitable downturns in order to participate in the superior long-term returns that, based on historical experience, a diversified portfolio of quality stocks will provide.

[Source: Dan Richards, Marketing Solutions]

I hope that in some small way this book contributes to your and your family's financial well-being.

Brent Bullis
June 1999

The Financial Planning Information Form

FAMILY INFORMATION

	SELF		**SPOUSE**	
FIRST NAME				
LAST NAME				
DATE OF BIRTH	AGE:	DATE OF BIRTH:		AGE:
S.I.N.	☐☐☐ ☐☐☐ ☐☐☐		☐☐☐ ☐☐☐ ☐☐☐	
HOME ADDRESS				
PHONE		POSTAL CODE		
EMPLOYER				
JOB TITLE				
BUS. PHONE				
HOBBIES				
SMOKER	YES ☐ NO ☐	YES ☐	NO ☐	

LIST ALL CHILDREN FOR ESTATE PLANNING PURPOSES

CHILD'S NAME	AGE
CHILD'S NAME	AGE
CHILD'S NAME	AGE
CHILD'S NAME	AGE
CHILD'S NAME	AGE

RETIREMENT FACTORS

At what age do you want to be financially
independent/retired?   _____

Once you have reached retirement, how
many years do you want your capital to last?   _____

Do you plan to downsize your home either at
or before retirement?   _____

If so, what price of home would you downsize
to, in today's dollars?   _____

Do you qualify for full or partial CPP benefits?
(if partial indicate amount)   _____

Does your spouse qualify for full or partial CPP
benefits? (if partial indicate amount)   _____

Estimated annual pay increase rate   _____ %

Estimated annual inflation rate   _____ %

Estimated annual increase rate for CPP & OAS   _____ %

Do you have wills?   Yes ☐   No ☐

When did you review them last?   _____

NOTES

_____

_____

ASSETS

Attach statements from Financial Institutions where you have investments
and/or RRSP(s).

	SELF	SPOUSE	JOINT	TOTAL
INCOME PRODUCING ASSETS				
BANK ACCOUNTS	_____	_____	_____	_____
T-BILLS, MONEY MARKET FUNDS	_____	_____	_____	_____
GICS, TERM DEPOSITS, CSBS	_____	_____	_____	_____
EQUITY MUTUAL FUNDS	_____	_____	_____	_____
BOND & MORTGAGE MUTUAL FUNDS	_____	_____	_____	_____

	SELF	SPOUSE	JOINT	TOTAL
REAL ESTATE MUTUAL FUNDS				
LIFE INSURANCE CASH VALUES				
STOCKS				
MORTGAGES HELD				
LOANS HELD				
RRIFS				
ANNUITIES				
TAX SHELTERS				
BUSINESS INTERESTS				
RENTAL PROPERTY				

RRSPs

	SELF	SPOUSE	JOINT	TOTAL
T-BILLS, MONEY MARKET FUNDS				
GICS, TERM DEPOSITS, CSBS				
EQUITY MUTUAL FUNDS				
BOND & MORTGAGE MUTUAL FUNDS				
REAL ESTATE MUTUAL FUNDS				
OTHER				

COMPANY PENSIONS

	SELF	SPOUSE	JOINT	TOTAL
COMPANY PENSION				
GROUP RRSP				
DEFERRED PROFIT SHARING				

NON-INCOME PRODUCING ASSETS

	SELF	SPOUSE	JOINT	TOTAL
HOME				
RECREATIONAL PROPERTY				
FURNISHINGS				
ART, ANTIQUES, COLLECTIBLES				
AUTOMOBILES				
RECREATIONAL VEHICLES				

NOTES

_____

_____

COMPANY PENSION PLANS

Attach Company Plan estimate or Pension Plan estimate if available.

	SELF	SPOUSE
REGISTERED PENSION PLANS		
PROJECTED PENSION AT RETIRED AGE	$	$
WILL PENSION BE INDEXED UPON RETIREMENT OR BASED ON YEARS OF SERVICE?		
CURRENT PENSIONABLE EARNINGS	$	$
AVERAGING PERIOD OVER HOW MANY YEARS?	YRS	YRS
YEARS OF SERVICE	YRS	YRS
PENSION RATE PERCENTAGE	%	%

ADDITIONAL DETAILS:

	SELF	SPOUSE
GROUP RRSP OR DPSP		
CURRENT VALUE		
MONTHLY DEPOSITS		
RATE OF RETURN DURING ACCUMULATION		
RATE OF RETURN AFTER MATURITY		
PAYOUT PERIOD OVER HOW MANY YEARS?		
INCOME		
EMPLOYMENT INCOME (BEFORE DEDUCTIONS)		
EMPLOYMENT INCOME (AFTER DEDUCTIONS)		
INCOME TAX PAID (ANNUALLY)		
MARGINAL TAX BRACKET		
BONUS (AFTER TAX)		
FAMILY ALLOWANCE (AFTER TAX)		
INTEREST INCOME (AFTER TAX)		
INVESTMENT INCOME (AFTER TAX)		

	SELF	SPOUSE	JOINT	TOTAL
ALIMONY (AFTER TAX)				
NET RENTAL INCOME (AFTER TAX)				

LIABILITIES

	SELF	SPOUSE	JOINT	TOTAL
HOUSE MORTGAGE				
RECREATIONAL PROPERTY MORTGAGE				
RENTAL PROPERTY MORTGAGE				
PERSONAL LOAN				
INVESTMENT LOAN				
AUTOMOBILE LOAN				
CREDIT CARDS				
BUSINESS LOANS				

The following chart outlines in detail typical sources of income and expenses families incur on an ongoing basis. We do not need your specific living expenses. The chart is included to assist you in calculating your required monthly income.

LIVING EXPENSES (OPTIONAL)

	ANNUAL CURRENT COSTS	ANNUAL RETIREMENT COSTS (TODAY'S)
PRINCIPAL RESIDENCE		
MORTGAGE/RENT		
PROPERTY TAX		
HEAT, HYDRO, & WATER		
LANDSCAPING COSTS		
GENERAL HOME REPAIR		
INTERIOR DECORATING		
FIRE & GENERAL INSURANCE		
TELEPHONE		
CONDO FEES		
TRANSPORTATION		
AUTO MAINTENANCE		
AUTO GASOLINE		

AUTO INSURANCE _____ _____

AUTO REPLACEMENT COSTS _____ _____

AUTO LICENSES _____ _____

PUBLIC TRANSPORTATION _____ _____

PERSONAL EXPENSES

SPENDING MONEY (WEEKLY X 52) _____ _____

CHILDREN'S ALLOWANCE _____ _____

HAIRDRESSER, BARBER _____ _____

PERSONAL CARE PRODUCTS _____ _____

ENTERTAINMENT

MOVIES, PLAYS _____ _____

CABLE TV _____ _____

CLUB & LODGE DUES _____ _____

SPORTS & HOBBY EQUIPMENT _____ _____

DINING & DANCING _____ _____

BABYSITTING FEE _____ _____

VACATIONS/TRAVEL _____ _____

NEWSPAPERS & MAGAZINES _____ _____

TELEPHONE _____ _____

CLOTHING & FOOTWEAR

YOU _____ _____

YOUR SPOUSE _____ _____

CHILDREN _____ _____

DRY CLEANING _____ _____

GROCERIES (WEEKLY X 52) _____ _____

HEALTH CARE

MEDICAL NEEDS & PRESCRIPTIONS _____ _____

DENTAL COSTS _____ _____

EYE CARE _____ _____

DONATIONS (CHURCH &

CHARITIES) _____ _____

PERSONAL INSURANCE _____ _____

LIFE INSURANCE _____ _____

DISABILITY INSURANCE _____ _____

HEALTH INSURANCE _____ _____

GIFTS (XMAS, BIRTH., ANN., WEDD.) _____ _____

UNIVERSITY & COLLEGE COSTS _____ _____

MISCELLANEOUS

CHILDCARE EXPENSES _____ _____

DOMESTIC HELP _____ _____

ALIMONY/CHILD SUPPORT _____ _____

PET FOOD _____ _____

PET MEDICAL COSTS _____ _____

WATER SOFTENER COSTS _____ _____

RECREATIONAL PROPERTY _____ _____

MORTGAGE/RENT/CONDO FEES _____ _____

PROPERTY TAXES _____ _____

HEAT, HYDRO, & WATER _____ _____

LANDSCAPING COSTS _____ _____

INTERIOR DECORATING _____ _____

FIRE & GENERAL INSURANCE _____ _____

TELEPHONE _____ _____

VERY IMPORTANT
Required Monthly Income in Today's Dollars
Upon Retirement (After Tax) _____

LIFE INSURANCE

NAME OF INSURED _____

COMPANY	POLICY NO.	ISSUE DATE	TYPE	FACE AMT.	PREMIUM
_____	_____	_____	_____	_____	_____
_____	_____	_____	_____	_____	_____
GROUP INSURANCE	_____	_____	_____	_____	_____
			TOTAL	_____	_____

NAME OF INSURED _____

_____	_____	_____	_____	_____	_____
_____	_____	_____	_____	_____	_____
GROUP INSURANCE	_____	_____	_____	_____	_____
			TOTAL	_____	_____

Do you have a shareholder/partner buy/sell agreement?   Yes ☐   No ☐

If yes, is it funded?   Yes ☐   No ☐

Would you require domestic help/childcare while
   raising the children?   Yes ☐   No ☐

What would you estimate the annual cost to be?   _____

Do you want to be able to continue saving for your
   retirement while raising your family?   _____

DISABILITY INSURANCE

NAME OF INSURED   _____

COMPANY	POLICY NO.	ISSUE DATE	TYPE	FACE AMT.	PREMIUM
GROUP INSURANCE					
		TOTAL			

NAME OF INSURED   _____

GROUP INSURANCE					
		TOTAL			

Do you want to maintain your standard of living
   in the event you become disabled?   Yes ☐   No ☐

Do you want to continue saving for your retirement
   if you are disabled?   Yes ☐   No ☐

NOTES

_____

_____

EDUCATION PLANNING

Do you want your children to attend University or College   Yes ☐   No ☐

Do you plan to assist them financially while they attend   Yes ☐   No ☐

Do you expect each child to contribute towards the cost
   of their education while attending University or College   Yes ☐   No ☐

NAME	YRS. UNTIL ATTENDING	NO. YRS. ATTENDING	1ST YR. COSTS TODAY'S $	INFLATION RATE ON COSTS	ANNUAL CONTRIB. BY CHILD TODAY'S $	INFLATION ON CHILD'S CONTRIB.	EXISTING $ FOR EDCUATION

LOAN DETAILS

LOAN TYPE	LOAN AMOUNT	INTEREST RATE	PAYMENT	TERM RENEWAL DATE	AMORT. PERIOD	LENDER	PREPAYMENT OPTIONS
HOME MORT.							
REC. PROP. MORT.							
AUTO							
PERSONAL							
CREDIT CARDS							
LINE OF CREDIT							
INVEST. LOAN							
BUSINESS LOAN							
OTHER							

NOTES

Investment And Regular Deposits

THE VALUE OF $100.00

Amount of initial investment	$100.00
Annual return	10.00%
Number of years	40
Amount of each deposit	$0.00
Deposit frequency	Monthly
Deposits to be made at	Beginning
Deposits increased annually by	0.00%

Annual Cash Flow

Period	Deposit per period	Total deposits	Growth	Estimated value
1	100.00	100.00	10.00	110.00
2	–	100.00	21.00	121.00
3	–	100.00	33.10	133.10
4	–	100.00	46.41	146.41
5	–	100.00	61.05	161.05
6	–	100.00	77.16	177.16
7	–	100.00	94.87	194.87
8	–	100.00	114.36	214.36
9	–	100.00	135.79	235.79
10	–	100.00	159.37	259.37
11	–	100.00	185.31	285.31
12	–	100.00	213.84	313.84
13	–	100.00	245.23	345.23
14	–	100.00	279.75	379.75

Annual Cash Flow (continued)

Period	Deposit per period	Total deposits	Growth	Estimated value
15	—	100.00	317.72	417.72
16	—	100.00	359.50	459.50
17	—	100.00	405.45	505.45
18	—	100.00	455.99	555.99
19	—	100.00	511.59	611.59
20	—	100.00	572.75	672.75
21	—	100.00	640.03	740.03
22	—	100.00	714.03	814.03
23	—	100.00	795.43	895.43
24	—	100.00	884.97	984.97
25	—	100.00	983.47	1,083.47
26	—	100.00	1,091.82	1,191.82
27	—	100.00	1,211.00	1,311.00
28	—	100.00	1,342.10	1,442.10
29	—	100.00	1,486.31	1,586.31
30	—	100.00	1.644.94	1,744.94
31	—	100.00	1,819.43	1,919.43
32	—	100.00	2,011.38	2,111.38
33	—	100.00	2,222.52	2,322.52
34	—	100.00	2,454.77	2,554.77
35	—	100.00	2,710.24	2,810.24
36	—	100.00	2,991.27	3,091.27
37	—	100.00	3,300.39	3,400.39
38	—	100.00	3,640.43	3,740.43
39	—	100.00	4,014.48	4,114.48
40	—	100.00	4,425.93	4,525.93
	Total	**100.00**	**4,425.93**	**4,525.93**

The information contained herein is based on certain assumptions and is for illustration purposes only. While care is taken in the preparation of this document, no warranty is made as to its accuracy or applicability in any particular case.

REGULAR DEPOSITS

Amount of initial investment	$0.00
Annual return	10.00%
Number of years	40
Amount of each deposit	$100.00
Deposit frequency	Monthly
Deposits to be made at	Beginning
Deposits increased annually by	00.00%

Annual Cash Flow

Period	Deposit per period	Total deposits	Growth	Estimated value
1	1,200.00	1,200.00	64.05	1,264.05
2	1,200.00	2,400.00	254.51	2,654.51
3	1,200.00	3,600.00	548.02	4,184.02
4	1,200.00	4,800.00	1,066.47	5,866.47
5	1,200.00	6,000.00	1,717.17	7,717.17
6	1,200.00	7,200.00	2,552.95	9,752.95
7	1,200.00	8,400.00	3,592.29	11,992.29
8	1,200.00	9,600.00	4,855.58	14,455.58
9	1,200.00	10,800.00	6,365.19	17,165.19
10	1,200.00	12,000.00	8,145.76	20,145.76
11	1,200.00	13,200.00	10,224.39	23,424.39
12	1,200.00	14,400.00	12,630.88	27,030.88
13	1,200.00	15,600.00	15,398.02	30,998.02
14	1,200.00	16,800.00	18,561.88	35,361.88
15	1,200.00	18,000.00	22,162.12	40,162.12
16	1,200.00	19,200.00	26,242.39	45,442.39
17	1,200.00	20,400.00	30,850.68	51,250.68
18	1,200.00	21,600.00	36,039.80	57,639.80
19	1,200.00	22,800.00	41,867.84	64,667.84
20	1,200.00	24,000.00	48,398.67	72,398.67
21	1,200.00	25,200.00	55,702.59	80,902.59
22	1,200.00	26,400.00	63,856.91	90,256.91
23	1,200.00	27,600.00	72,946.65	100,546.65
24	1,200.00	28,800.00	83,065.37	111,865.37
25	1,200.00	30,000.00	94,315.96	124,315.96
26	1,200.00	31,200.00	106,811.61	138,011.61
27	1,200.00	32,400.00	120,676.83	153,076.83
28	1,200.00	33,600.00	136,048.56	169,648.56
29	1,200.00	34,800.00	153,077.47	187,877.47
30	1,200.00	36,000.00	171,929.27	207,929.27

Annual Cash Flow (continued)

Period	Deposit per period	Total deposits	Growth	Estimated value
31	1,200.00	37,200.00	192,786.25	229,986.25
32	1,200.00	38,400.00	215,848.93	254,248.93
33	1,200.00	39,600.00	241,337.88	280,937.88
34	1,200.00	40,800.00	269,495.72	310,295.72
35	1,200.00	42,000.00	300,589.35	342,589.35
36	1,200.00	43,200.00	334,912.33	378,112.33
37	1,200.00	44,400.00	372,787.62	417,187.62
38	1,200.00	45,600.00	414,570.44	460,170.44
39	1,200.00	46,800.00	460,651.53	507,451.53
40	1,200.00	48,000.00	511,460.74	559,460.74
Total		**48,000.00**	**511,460.74**	**559,460.74**

The information contained herein is based on certain assumptions and is for illustration purposes only. While care is taken in the preparation of this document, no warranty is made as to its accuracy or applicability in any particular case.

The Infinity International, Canadian, and Wealth Management Funds

INFINITY INTERNATIONAL FUND					
Statement of Investment Portfolio					
As at December 31, 1998 (unaudited)					
		Amount invested: $100,000			
				PERFORMANCE†	
Equities	%	Breakdown ($)	5-year	10-year	15-year
American Express Co.*	4.0%	4,000	21%	11%	10%
Berkshire Hathaway Inc., Class A *	10.1%	10,100	31%	30%	30%
Coca-Cola Co. *	4.8%	4,800	26%	30%	26%
Exxon Corp.	0.9%	900	13%	12%	14%
Fairfax Financial Holdings Ltd. *	1.7%	1,700	67%	37%	38%
Federal Home and Loan Mortgage Corp.	3.5%	3,500	21%		
Franklin Resources, Inc. *	3.1%	3,100	29%	30%	54%
Gannett Co., Inc.	2.4%	2,400	11%	8%	10%
General Electric Co.	1.7%	1,700	21%	18%	16%
Gillette Co. *	6.2%	6,200	29%	30%	27%
Johnson & Johnson *	2.4%	2,400	19%	21%	16%
McDonald's Corp.	3.1%	3,100	17%	17%	18%
Mellon Bank Corp. *	1.1%	1,100	19%	17%	8%
Merck & Co., Inc.	3.5%	3,500	16%	18%	22%
Merrill Lynch & Co., Inc	3.6%	3,600	35%	28%	11%
Microsoft Corp. *	5.5%	5,500	43%	93%	
Nike	1.3%	1,300	32%	41%	27%
Procter & Gamble Co. *	4.6%	4,600	43%	23%	12%
T. Rowe Price Associates *	2.3%	2,300	44%	29%	
Trimark Financial Corp. *	2.3%	2,300	77%		

		Amount invested: $100,000			
			PERFORMANCE[†]		
Equities	**%**	**Breakdown ($)**	**5-year**	**10-year**	**15-year**
Wal-Mart	0.8%	800	-4%	14%	23%
Walt Disney Co. *	5.2%	5,200	18%	21%	24%
Washington Post co.	0.9%	900	9%	7%	13%
Wells Fargo & Co. *	5.4%	5,400	35%	23%	24%
Wesco Financial Corp.	1.2%	1,200	36%	25%	19%
Wm. Wrigley Jr. Co.	2.7%	2,700	12%	18%	24%
Cash and other net assets	15.7%	15,700			
Total net assets	**100.0%**	**Total amount invested: $100,000**			

*Equity held in more than one fund
[†]Performance based on December 31, 1997, returns excluding dividends.

INFINITY CANADIAN FUND
Statement of Investment Portfolio
As at December 31, 1998 (unaudited)

Equities	%	Amount invested: $100,000 Breakdown ($)	PERFORMANCE† 5-year	10-year	15-year
AGF Management Limited, Class B *	2.1%	2,100	41%	20%	29%
Aetna Inc.	0.3%	300	14%	7%	6%
American Express Company *	0.3%	300	21%	11%	10%
Bank of Montreal	1.1%	1,100	19%	15%	10%
Bank of Nova Scotia	1.0%	1,000	20%	16%	11%
Berkshire Hathaway Inc., Class A *	4.4%	4,400	31%	30%	30%
Bombardier Inc., Class B	4.8%	4,800	37%	32%	32%
BPI Financial Corp. *	0.0%	0	N/A	N/A	N/A
Canadian Imperial Bank of Commerce	1.3%	1,300	20%	13%	10%
CanWest Global Comm. Corp., Class S	4.5%	4,500	54%		
Coca-Cola Company *	2.6%	2,600	26%	30%	26%
Dundee Bancorp Inc., Class A *	0.8%	800			
Fairfax Financial Holdings Ltd. *	4.5%	4,500	67%	37%	38%
Franco-Nevada Mining Corp	3.0%	3,000	41%	35%	45%[,2]
Gillette Company *	2.7%	2,700	29%	30%	27%
Infinity Income Trust	0.1%	100			
Investor Group Inc.	0.8%	800	23%	13%	
Johnson & Johnson *	1.0%	1,000	19%	21%	16%
Loblaw Companies Ltd.	5.1%	5,100	32%	22%	15%
Loewen Group Inc.	0.5%	500	19%	31%	
Mackenzie Financial Corp. *	5.3%	5,300	25%	16%	27%
Magna Int'l Inc., Class A	3.3%	3,300	23%	24%	14%
MDS Inc., Class A	0.0%	0			
MDS Inc., Class B	1.7%	1,700			
Microsoft Corp. *	2.0%	2,000	43%	93%	
Montrusco Associates Inc. *	0.2%	200			
Newcourt Credit Group	6.3%	6,300	56%[1]		
Power Financial Corp. *	5.1%	5,100	37%	22%	30%[2]
Procter & Gamble Company *	1.1%	1,100	43%	23%	12%
Royal Bank of Canada	1.8%	1,800	25%	18%	12%
Sceptre Investment Counsel Ltd., Class A	0.9%	900	33%	30%	
Thomson Corp.	6.4%	6,400	22%		
Toronto-Dominion Bank	1.6%	1,600	23%	13%	18%
Trimark Financial Corp. *	4.4%	4,400	77%		
Wal-Mart	0.6%	600	-4%	14%	23%
Walt Disney Company *	1.8%	1,800	18%	21%	24%

Equities	%	Amount invested: $100,000 Breakdown ($)	PERFORMANCE† 5-year	10-year	15-year
Wells Fargo & Company *	1.8%	1,800	35%	23%	24%
Cash and other net assets	14.8%	14,800			
Total net assets	100.0%	Total amount invested: $100,000			

*Equity held in more than one fund
†Performance based on December 31, 1997, returns excluding dividends.
¹Based on 3-year average
²Based on 14-year average

INFINITY WEALTH MANAGEMENT FUND
Statement of Investment Portfolio
As at December 31, 1998 (unaudited)

Amount invested: $100,000

Equities	%	Breakdown ($)	5-year	10-year	15-year
AGF Management Ltd., Class B *	6.7%	6,700	33%	16%	29%
Bank of Montreal	0.5%	500	19%	15%	10%
BPI Financial Corp. *	0.2%	200			
Canadian Imperial Bank of Commerce	0.6%	600	20%	13%	10%
C.I. Fund Management Inc.	2.9%	2,900			
Citigroup Inc.	1.5%	1,500	N/A	N/A	N/A
Dundee Bancorp. Inc., Class A *	2.2%	2,200	60%		
Fairfax Financial Holdings Ltd. *	5.2%	5,200	67%	37%	38%
Franklin Resources, Inc. *	2.7%	2,700	29%	30%	54%
Guardian Capital Group Ltd., Class A	1.8%	1,800			
Investors Group Inc.	8.7%	8,700	23%	13%	
J.P. Morgan *	1.8%	1,800	13%	10%	15%
Mackenzie Financial Corp. *	8.7%	8,700	25%	16%	27%
Mellon Bank Corp. *	2.7%	2,700	19%	17%	8%
Merrill Lynch *	2.3%	2,300	35%	28%	11%
Montrusco Associates Inc. *	0.4%	400			
Perigee	0.5%	500			
Perpetual PLC	0.7%	700			
Power Financial Corp. *	9.8%	9,800	37%	22%	30%
Royal Bank of Canada *	5.0%	5,000	25%	18%	12%
Sceptre Investment Counsel Ltd., Class A *	3.2%	3,200	33%	30%	
Scotiabank	0.4%	400	20%	16%	11%
Swiss Reinsurance (ADR)	2.3%	2,300			
T. Rowe Price Associates *	3.5%	3,500	44%	29%	
Toronto Dominion Bank *	4.2%	4,200	23%	13%	18%
Trimark Financial Corp. *	6.6%	6,600	77%		
Cash and other net assets	14.9%	14,900			
Total net assets	100.0%	Total amount invested: $100,000			

*Equity held in more than one fund
†Performance based on December 31, 1997, returns excluding dividends.
¹Based on 14-year average

Request for a Reduction of Tax Deductions at Source

Personal Information   ☐ Client   ☐ Spouse

FIRST NAME: _____   SIN: _____

LAST NAME: _____   PHONE (W): _____

ADDRESS: _____   PHONE (H): _____

EMPLOYER/PAYER: _____

ADDRESS: _____

CONTACT PERSON: _____   PHONE: _____

I hereby request authorization for my employer/payer to reduce income tax deductions at source as I anticipate the following deductions for the year ending December 31, _____ .

1. **Alimony/Child Support Payments** $ _____ /Yr

    Attach a copy of the court order or written separation agreement if not previously provided or if it has been amended.

    Note: If you are claiming *only* alimony/child support payments you may request authorization for up to five years. (A copy of the court order or written separation agreement MUST accompany your request.) Indicate the years you are requesting authorization for: _____

2. **Registered Retirement Savings Plan Contributions** $ _____ /Yr

    (Do not include Home Buyer's Plan Repayments)

    As your allowable contributions are based on prior year earned income and Pension Adjustment amount, provide sufficient information to estimate your RRSP deduction room. (For example, if your request is for the year 2000, provide 1999 earned income and Pension Adjustment (PA) Amount or a copy of the 1999 T4 slip.)

Earned Income (Box 14 - T4)   P.A. Amount (Box 52 - T4)

Prior year: $ _____   Prior year: $ _____

Current year: $ _____   Current year: $ _____

Is your RRSP contribution offsetting a lump sum payment (i.e., a non-eligible portion of a retiring allowance or vacation pay)? Yes ☐   No ☐

If "Yes," indicate the type of payment _____

3. **Limited Partnership Loss; Tax Shelters;**
   Flow-Through Shares $ _____   /Yr

   If you have not claimed this in the past or this is a new investment, provide copies of the Prospectus, Subscription Agreement, and Proof of Payment.

4. **Minimum Tax Carry Forward** $ _____   /Yr

   Provide a complete Form T691, Calculation of Minimum Tax.

5. **Interest and Carrying Charges on Investments** $ _____ /Yr

   Provide the following:

   - a statement from the lender(s) showing the date of the loan, amount of the loan, and estimated interest payable for the year.
   - documentation to support that the loan was used for investment purposes.

6. **Child Care Expenses** $ _____   /Yr

   Provide the following:

   - Spouse's net income $ _____
   - Number of children   _____
   - Birthdate(s) of child(ren): _____   _____

                                  _____   _____

                                  _____   _____

                                  _____   _____

7. **Charitable Donations** $ _____   /Yr

8. **Oil and Gas (C.E.E., C.D.E., and C.O.G.P.E.)** $ _____ /Yr

   Provide copies of the Prospectus, Subscription Agreement, and Proof of Payment. If this is a carryover of C.E.E. and/or C.D.E., provide the carry forward schedule.

9. **Automobile Expenses** $ _____ /Yr

Provide a breakdown of expenses or a completed Form T777, Statement of Employment Expenses.

10. **Certified Films** $ _____ /Yr

Provide copies of the Prospectus, Subscription Agreement, Proof of Payment, and Certificate from the Minister of Canadian Heritage.

11. **Other (i.e., Rental Loss, Business Loss)** $ _____ /Yr

Please provide details and supporting documentation.

Total Deductions $ _____ /Yr

*Note, if total deductions exceed $40,000 you may be subject to a minimum tax and should complete From T691, Calculation of Minimum Tax.

Statement of Estimated Income From All Sources in _____**(year)**

Salary/bonuses, etc.	$_____	/Yr
Commission income	$_____	/Yr
Interest and other investment income	$_____	/Yr
Dividends from taxable Canadian corporations	$_____	/Yr
Taxable capital gains	$_____	/Yr
Net rental income (loss)	$_____	/Yr
Self-employed income	$_____	/Yr
Other income (please specify)	$_____	/Yr
Total Estimated Income From All Sources	$ _____	/Yr

I certify that the information given in this statement is true, correct, and complete to the best of my knowledge and belief.

I am aware that a waiver is granted based on estimates and that I am liable for all taxes owing upon assessment.

Date: _____ Signature: _____

Please submit completed Form "E" to your local Client Services Division, Revenue Canada.

Saving $1,000 a Year Versus Borrowing $25,000 to Invest

INVESTMENT AND REGULAR DEPOSITS

Amount of initial investment	$0.00
Annual return	10.00%
Number of years	25
Amount of each deposit	$1,000.00
Deposit frequency	Annually
Deposits to be made at	End
Deposits increased annually by	00.00%

Annual Cash Flow

Period	Deposit per period	Total deposits	Growth	Estimated value
1	1,000.00	1,000.00	–	1,000.00
2	1,000.00	2,000.00	100.00	2,100.00
3	1,000.00	3,000.00	310.00	3,310.00
4	1,000.00	4,000.00	641.00	4,641.00
5	1,000.00	5,000.00	1,105.10	6,105.10
6	1,000.00	6,000.00	1,715.61	7,715.61
7	1,000.00	7,000.00	2,487.17	9,487.17
8	1,000.00	8,000.00	3,435.89	11,435.89
9	1,000.00	9,000.00	4,579.48	13,579.48
10	1,000.00	10,000.00	5,937.42	15,937.42
11	1,000.00	11,000.00	7,531.17	18,531.17
12	1,000.00	12,000.00	9,384.28	21,384.28
13	1,000.00	13,000.00	11,522.71	24,522.71
14	1,000.00	14,000.00	13,974.98	27,974.98

Annual Cash Flow (continued)

Period	Deposit per period	Total deposits	Growth	Estimated value
15	1,000.00	15,000.00	16,772.48	31,772.48
16	1,000.00	16,000.00	19,949.73	35,949.73
17	1,000.00	17,000.00	23,544.70	40,544.70
18	1,000.00	18,000.00	27,599.17	45,599.17
19	1,000.00	19,000.00	32,159.09	51,159.05
20	1,000.00	20,000.00	37,275.00	57,275.00
21	1,000.00	21,000.00	43,002.50	64,002.50
22	1,000.00	22,000.00	49,402.75	71,402.75
23	1,000.00	23,000.00	56,543.02	79,543.02
24	1,000.00	24,000.00	64,497.33	88,497.33
25	1,000.00	25,000.00	73,347.06	98,347.06
Total		**25,000.00**	**73,347.06**	**98,347.06**

LEVERAGE PLAN

Amount borrowed	$25,000
Rate of return	10.00%
Average loan interest rate	8.00%
Marginal income tax rate	50.00%
After-tax interest rate	4.00%

Annual Cash Flow

Year	Opening balance	Annual gain	Before-tax interest paid	Net after-tax interest paid	SWP 0.00%	Closing balance
1	25,000	2,500	2,000	1,000	–	27,500
2	27,500	2,750	2,000	1,000	–	30,250
3	30,250	3,025	2,000	1,000	–	33,275
4	33,275	3,328	2,000	1,000	–	36,603
5	36,603	3,660	2,000	1,000	–	40,263
6	40,263	4,026	2,000	1,000	–	44,289
7	44,289	4,429	2,000	1,000	–	48,718
8	48,718	4,872	2,000	1,000	–	53,590
9	53,590	5,359	2,000	1,000	–	58,949
10	58,949	5,895	2,000	1,000	–	64,844
11	64,844	6,484	2,000	1,000	–	71,328
12	71,328	7,133	2,000	1,000	–	78,461
13	78,461	7,846	2,000	1,000	–	86,307
14	86,307	8,631	2,000	1,000	–	94,937
15	94,937	9,494	2,000	1,000	–	104,431
16	104,431	10,443	2,000	1,000	–	114,874
17	114,874	11,487	2,000	1,000	–	126,362
18	126,362	12,636	2,000	1,000	–	138,998
19	138,998	13,900	2,000	1,000	–	152,898
20	152,898	15,290	2,000	1,000	–	168,187
21	168,187	16,819	2,000	1,000	–	185,006
22	185,006	18,501	2,000	1,000	–	203,507
23	203,507	20,351	2,000	1,000	–	223,858
24	223,858	22,386	2,000	1,000	–	246,243
25	246,243	24,624	2,000	1,000	–	270,868

*Interest paid from other income sources.
Figures quoted are only projections and are not guarantees of future performance.

The Family Tax Strategy

PERSONAL INFORMATION:

Mr. Client	Age: 40
Mrs. Client	Age: 40

INVESTMENT INFORMATION:

Annual deposit	$5,000
Number of years to deposit	5
Projected investment rate of return	8.20%
Marginal income tax rate	46.00%
Compound annual return — after tax	4.40%
Annual withdrawal	$15,000
Year annual withdrawal to start	25
Projected bank loan rate	8.05%

HOW IT WORKS

REGULAR INVESTMENT		FAMILY TAX STRATEGY	
STEP #1		STEP #1	
Amount of annual desposit	$5,000	Amount of annual deposit	$5,000
Number of years to deposit	5	Number of years to deposit	5
Number of years additional growth	19	Number years additional growth	19
Before-tax rate of return	8.2%	Before- and after-tax rate of return	8.2%
After-tax rate of return	4.4%		
Value	*$64,972*	*Value*	*$153,413*

COMPARISON — Regular Investment vs. FTS (see charts on the following pages)

You have an investment advantage using the FTS of	$88,441
Life insurance included with FTS	$285,185

STEP #2		STEP #2	
Annual amount to withdraw	$15,000	Income (amount borrowed)	$15,000
Year withdrawals to start	25	Year income to start	25
Year withdrawals to end	28		
Number of withdrawals	4	Number of withdrawals	4
		Value	*$153,154*
		Plus insurance	*$329,825*
Total value remaining	*$13,163*	Total value	*$482,979*

SUMMARY

The FTS will permit you to reduce your investment risk and increase your portfolio value.

The value of your estate will be increased by: $469,816

REGULAR INVESTMENT

Year	Annual deposit	Growth	Income (withdrawals)	Year end balance
1	5,000	221	–	5,221
2	5,000	453	–	10,674
3	5,000	694	–	16,368
4	5,000	946	–	22,314
5	5,000	1,209	–	28,524
6	–	1,263	–	29,787
7	–	1,319	–	31,106
8	–	1,377	–	32,483
9	–	1,438	–	33,921
10	–	1,502	–	35,423
11	–	1,569	–	36,992
12	–	1,638	–	38,630
13	–	1,711	–	40,341
14	–	1,786	–	42,127
15	–	1,865	–	43,992
16	–	1,948	–	45,940
17	–	2,034	–	47,974
18	–	2,124	–	50,099
19	–	2,218	–	52,317
20	–	2,317	–	54,634
21	–	2,419	–	57,053
22	–	2,526	–	59,579
23	–	2,638	–	62,217
24	–	2,755	–	64,972
25	–	2,877	15,000	52,849
26	–	2,340	15,000	40,189
27	–	1,780	15,000	26,969
28	–	1,194	15,000	13,163

FAMILY TAX STRATEGY

Year	Income (amount borrowed)	Accumulated loan	Loan maximum (80% of CSV)	Cash surrender value	Death benefit	FTS value
1	–	–	3,017	3,771	286,626	286,626
2	–	–	6,366	7,958	291,770	291,770
3	–	–	10,073	12,591	297,361	297,361
4	–	–	14,169	17,711	303,438	303,438
5	–	–	19,815	24,769	325,633	325,633
6	–	–	21,704	27,130	297,225	297,225
7	–	–	24,583	30,729	288,572	288,572
8	–	–	27,692	34,615	284,430	284,430
9	–	–	31,050	38,813	283,493	283,493
10	–	–	34,681	43,351	284,971	284,971
11	–	–	37,842	47,303	282,681	282,681
12	–	–	41,335	51,669	283,041	283,041
13	–	–	45,188	56,485	285,622	285,622
14	–	–	49,438	61,797	290,160	290,160
15	–	–	54,119	67,649	296,463	296,463
16	–	–	59,265	74,081	304,357	304,357
17	–	–	64,914	81,143	313,763	313,763
18	–	–	71,111	88,889	324,621	324,621
19	–	–	77,899	97,374	336,891	336,891
20	–	–	85,334	106,667	350,591	350,591
21	–	–	93,466	116,833	370,757	370,757
22	–	–	102,362	127,952	392,094	392,094
23	–	–	112,082	140,102	414,640	414,650
24	–	–	122,730	153,413	438,598	438,598
25	15,000	15,000	134,399	167,999	464,047	449,047
26	15,000	31,200	147,196	183,995	491,124	459,924
27	15,000	48,696	161,214	201,518	519,911	471,215
28	15,000	67,592	176,597	220,746	550,571	482,979
29	15,000	87,999	193,461	241,826	583,234	495,235
30	15,000	110,039	211,950	264,937	618,016	507,977
31	15,000	133,842	232,221	290,276	655,072	521,230
32	15,000	159,549	254,452	318,065	694,602	535,053
33	15,000	187,313	278,793	348,491	736,674	549,361
34	15,000	217,298	305,412	381,765	781,409	564,111
35	15,000	249,682	334,448	418,060	828,826	579,144
36	15,000	284,657	366,116	457,645	879,088	594,431
37	15,000	322,429	400,575	500,719	932,265	609,836
38	15,000	363,224	438,070	547,588	988,550	625,326
39	15,000	407,282	478,865	598,581	1,048,156	640,874
40	15,000	454,864	523,214	654,018	1,111,293	656,429

The Systematic Withdrawal Plan

THE TRIMARK FUND SYSTEMATIC WITHDRAWAL PLAN

$100,000 PURCHASE

FOR THE PERIOD ENDING DECEMBER 31, 1998

This is an example of a *Trimark Systematic Withdrawal Plan*. The purchaser of the Plan invested $100,000 at the inception of Trimark Fund on September 1, 1981, and withdrew $833 each month, beginning on October 1, 1981.

The Trimark Fund account value reflects an initial deduction of a 4% commission as well as changes in unit value, and assumes income and capital gains distributions are reinvested. It does not take into account administrative fees, payable by unitholders, which would have reduced returns.

For comparative purposes, we have shown the same schedule of withdrawals at an 8% annual compounded rate of return with no fees deducted.

One-year, three-year, five-year, ten-year and fifteen-year historical annual compounded rates of return for Trimark Fund to December 31, 1998 were 6.4%, 12.3%, 13.7%, 15.8% and 14.8% respectively. Since its inception, investors in Trimark Fund have earned 17.2%. While all results are based on the past performance of the Fund, these are not necessarily indicative of future results. Your unit value and investment returns will fluctuate.

Date	Total annual withdrawal	=	Return of capital	+	Capital gain (loss)	Cumulative total withdrawals	Distributions reinvested each year	Annual tax liability at 40%*	Trimark Fund account value	Comparative plan value at 8% return	Annual tax liability at 40%*
Sep. 1/81	—		—		—	—	—	—	96,000	100,000	—
Dec. 31/81	2,500		2,559		(59)	2,500	—	—	98,594	100,133	1,053
Dec. 31/82	10,000		9,567		433	12,500	1,350	426	122,658	97,711	3,031
Dec. 31/83	10,000		6,054		3,946	22,500	15,743	4,043	155,045	95,094	2,953
Dec. 31/84	10,000		6,647		3,353	32,500	5,944	2,016	146,443	92,268	2,870
Dec. 31/85	10,000		5,844		4,156	42,500	1,376	384	189,115	89,217	2,779
Dec. 31/86	10,000		4,561		5,439	52,500	19,387	675	198,525	85,921	2,682
Dec. 31/87	10,000		4,897		5,103	62,500	31,841	744	185,303	82,361	2,576
Dec. 31/88	10,000		6,374		3,626	72,500	23,514	1,098	216,911	78,516	2,462
Dec. 31/89	10,000		6,221		3,779	82,500	18,287	1,766	241,192	74,364	2,339
Dec. 31/90	10,000		7,201		2,799	92,500	24,894	8,340	207,814	69,880	2,206
Dec. 31/91	10,000		7,507		2,493	102,500	3,619	1,827	255,558	65,037	2,063
Dec. 31/92	10,000		6,213		3,787	112,500	6,570	3,107	318,264	59,807	1,908
Dec. 31/93	10,000		5,054		4,946	122,500	26,744	9,507	406,993	54,158	1,740
Dec. 31/94	10,000		4,597		5,403	132,500	13,777	5,754	457,049	48,057	1,560
Dec. 31/95	10,000		4,309		5,691	142,500	29,677	10,610	522,220	41,469	1,365

Date	Total annual withdrawal	=	Return of capital	+	Capital gain (loss)	Cumulative total withdrawals	Distribtions reinvested each year	Annual tax liability at 40%*	Trimark Fund account value	Comparative plan value at 8% return	Annual tax liability at 40%*
Dec. 31/96	10,000		4,242		5,758	152,500	6,941	3,810	588,239	34,353	1,154
Dec. 31/97	10,000		3,672		6,328	162,500	131,522	41,520	671,799	26,668	926
Dec. 31/98	10,000		5,304		4,696	172,500	13,827	5,545	714,488	18,368	680

FUND PERFORMANCE

If you invested $100,000 in Trimark Fund on September 1, 1981, and withdrew $833 every month, you would have withdrawn a total of $172,500 and would still have $714,488 left.

If you withdrew the same amount from an investment earning 8%, you would have $18,368 left.

Important information about any mutual fund is contained in its simplified prospectus. Read your prospectus carefully before investing. Copies of Trimark's prospectus are available from your financial adviser or from Trimark Investment Management Inc.

*Tax liability assumes full access to the $100,000 lifetime captial gains exemption since 1985 until the $100,000 limit was reached in 1989 and also assumes that the $100,000 was not borrowed because CNIL would then apply.

THE TEMPLETON GROWTH FUND SYSTEMATIC WITHDRAWAL PLAN

Summary information of ten-year cash withdrawal programs based on
assumed net investments of $100,000 with monthly withdrawals of $833.33 ($10,000 each year).
a withdrawal of $10,000 per year — 10% of initial investmentment

From May 1	to April 30	Initial net investment	Capital gains dividends reinvested	Income dividends reinvested	Amount withdrawn in 10 years	Value at end of period
1955	1965	100,000	—	959	100,000.00	93,492
1956	1966	100,000	—	1,846	100,000.00	75,400
1957	1967	100,000	—	4,801	100,000.00	115,823
1958	1968	100,000	—	10,139	100,000.00	200,694
1959	1969	100,000	—	7,383	100,000.00	130,498
1069	1970	100,000	—	11,223	100,000.00	159,138
1961	1971	100,000	—	8,994	100,000.00	88,633
1962	1972	100,000	1,710	11,404	100,000.00	127,798
1963	1973	100,000	6,497	17,254	100,000.00	250,832
1964	1974	100,000	29,205	19,326	100,000.00	199,605
1965	1975	100,000	21,281	15,955	100,000.00	144,888
1966	1976	100,000	21,750	16,196	100,000.00	163,419

From May 1	to April 30	Initial net investment	Capital gains dividends reinvested	Income dividends reinvested	Amount withdrawn in 10 years	Value at end of period
1967	1977	100,000	27,082	18,818	100,000.00	248,971
1968	1978	100,000	38,610	19,191	100,000.00	316,202
1969	1979	100,000	28,719	14,937	100,000.00	239,018
1970	1980	100,000	35,753	18,514	100,000.00	298,994
1971	1981	100,000	58,927	24,950	100,000.00	458,967
1972	1982	100,000	51,672	22,774	100,000	267,364
1973	1983	100,000	37,477	20,233	100,000.00	233,673
1974	1984	100,000	38,878	32,974	100,000.00	385,811
1975	1985	100,000	52,147	41,264	100,000.00	462,214
1976	1986	100,000	64,779	44,869	100,000.00	557,325
1977	1987	100,000	69,734	45,317	100,000.00	449,308
1978	1988	100,000	46,069	29,922	100,000.00	249,046
1979	1989	100,000	45,166	28,822	100,000.00	248,915
1980	1990	100,000	44,609	27,600	100,000.00	227,693
1981	1991	100,000	29,554	18,825	100,000.00	139,595

From May 1	to April 30	Initial net investment	Capital gains dividends reinvested	Income dividends reinvested	Amount withdrawn in 10 years	Value at end of period
1982	1992	100,000	48,769	23,984	100,000.00	251,309
1983	1993	100,000	41,284	14,960	100,000.00	168,456
1984	1994	100,000	46,284	12,504	100,000.00	194,123
1985	1995	100,000	44,499	9,663	100,000.00	165,251

The Plan: The Registered Family Tax Strategy

PERSONAL INFORMATION:

Client   Age: 35

INVESTMENT INFORMATION:

Annual RRSP deposit	$4,000
Annual non-registered deposit	$1,000
Number of years to deposit — to age 55	20
Age to RRIF	69
Projected investment rate of return	8.00%
Amount of term-to-100 Insurance	$100,000
Term-to-100 annual premium	427.00
Number of years to pay T-100 premium	Life

BUY TERM & INVEST THE DIFFERENCE VERSUS THE PLAN

BUY TERM & INVEST THE DIFFERENCE AT AGE 55		THE PLAN AT AGE 55	
RRSP	197,692	RRSP	242,768
Insurance	100,000	Insurance	100,000
Investment account	28,319	Investment account	42,283
Total value	*326,011*	*Total value*	*385,051*
Total dollars invested	*100,000*	*Total dollars invested*	*100,000*

RRIF TIME — AGE 69		RRIF TIME — AGE 69	
RRSP to RRIF	580,659	RRSP to RRIF	901,584
Insurance	100,000	Insurance	100,000
Investment account	84,738	Investment account	136,110
Total value	*765,396*	*Total value*	*1,137,694*
Total dollars invested	*105,978*	*Total dollars invested*	*100,000*

LIFE INSURANCE		LIFE INSURANCE	
Premiums payable to	Age 100	Years premiums payable	20
Coverage	Age 100	Coverage	Age 100

Please refer to the next two pages of this appendix for a breakdown of how these numbers were calculated.

This proposal is for illustration purposes only. Figures quoted within are only projections and are not guarantees of future performance.

BUY TERM &
INVEST THE DIFFERENCE

Year	Age	RRSP deposit	RRSP account	Term insurance premium	Life insurance	Investment deposit	Growth	Investment account
1	36	4,000	4,320	427	100,000	573	46	619
2	37	4,000	8,986	427	100,000	573	141	1,287
3	38	4,000	14,024	427	100,000	573	290	2,009
4	39	4,000	19,466	427	100,000	573	497	2,789
5	40	4,000	25,344	427	100,000	573	765	3,630
6	41	4,000	31,691	427	100,000	573	1,102	4,540
7	42	4,000	38,547	427	100,000	573	1,511	5,522
8	43	4,000	45,950	427	100,000	573	1,998	6,582
9	44	4,000	53,946	427	100,000	573	2,571	7,728
10	45	4,000	62,582	427	100,000	573	3,235	8,965
11	46	4,000	71,909	427	100,000	573	3,998	10,301
12	47	4,000	81,981	427	100,000	573	4,868	11,744
13	48	4,000	92,860	427	100,000	573	5,853	13,302
14	49	4,000	104,608	427	100,000	573	6,963	14,985
15	50	4,000	117,297	427	100,000	573	8,208	16,803
16	51	4,000	131,001	427	100,000	573	9,598	18,766
17	52	4,000	145,801	427	100,000	573	11,145	20,886
18	53	4,000	161,785	427	100,000	573	12,862	23,176
19	54	4,000	179,048	427	100,000	573	14,762	25,649
20	55	4,000	197,692	427	100,000	573	16,859	28,319
21	56	—	213,507	427	100,000	—	19,125	31,158
22	57	—	230,588	427	100,000	—	21,618	33,651
23	58	—	249,035	427	100,000	—	24,310	36,343
24	59	—	268,957	427	100,000	—	27,217	39,250
25	60	—	290,474	427	100,000	—	30,357	42,390
26	61	—	313,712	427	100,000	—	33,748	45,781
27	62	—	338,809	427	100,000	—	37,411	49,444
28	63	—	365,914	427	100,000	—	41,366	53,399
29	64	—	395,187	427	100,000	—	45,638	57,671
30	65	—	426,802	427	100,000	—	50,252	62,285
31	66	—	460,946	427	100,000	—	55,235	67,268
32	67	—	497,821	427	100,000	—	60,616	72,649
33	68	—	537,647	427	100,000	—	66,428	78,461
34	69	—	580,659	427	100,000	—	72,705	84,738
35	70	—	627,111	427	100,000	—	79,484	91,517
36	71	—	677,280	427	100,000	—	86,805	98,838
37	72	—	731,463	427	100,000	—	94,712	106,745
38	73	—	789,980	427	100,000	—	103,252	115,285
39	74	—	853,178	427	100,000	—	112,474	124,507
40	75	—	921,432	427	100,000	—	122,435	134,468

THE PLAN

Year	Age	Non-registered deposit	Death benefit	Total cash value	Annual RRSP deposit	RRSP account
1	36	1,000	105,116	4,637	4,000	4,320
2	37	1,000	110,643	9,685	4,000	8,986
3	38	1,000	116,612	15,175	4,000	14,024
4	39	1,000	123,059	21,143	4,000	19,466
5	40	1,000	130,530	28,614	4,000	25,772
6	41	1,000	138,734	36,818	4,000	32,697
7	42	1,000	147,741	46,304	4,000	40,303
8	43	1,000	157,624	56,666	4,000	48,655
9	44	1,000	168,466	67,987	4,000	57,829
10	45	1,000	180,358	80,358	4,000	67,903
11	46	1,000	193,396	93,396	4,000	78,968
12	47	1,000	207,692	107,692	4,000	91,119
13	48	1,000	223,363	123,363	4,000	104,465
14	49	1,000	240,551	140,551	4,000	119,121
15	50	1,000	259,397	159,397	4,000	135,218
16	51	1,000	280,078	180,078	4,000	152,896
17	52	1,000	302,775	202,775	4,000	172,311
18	53	1,000	327,689	227,689	4,000	193,633
19	54	1,000	355,031	255,031	4,000	217,050
20	55	1,000	385,051	285,051	4,000	242,768
21	56	—	412,533	312,533	—	266,620
22	57	—	442,698	342,698	—	292,816
23	58	—	475,807	375,807	—	321,585
24	59	—	512,153	412,153	—	353,180
25	60	—	552,038	452,038	—	387,880
26	61	—	595,799	495,799	—	425,989
27	62	—	643,791	543,791	—	467,842
28	63	—	696,426	596,426	—	513,807
29	64	—	754,132	654,132	—	564,288
30	65	—	817,401	717,401	—	619,729
31	66	—	886,773	786,773	—	680,617
32	67	—	962,828	862,828	—	747,488
33	68	—	1,046,211	946,211	—	820,928
34	69	—	1,137,694	1,037,694	—	901,584
35	70	—	247,845	147,845	—	—
36	71	—	260,593	160,593	—	—
37	72	—	274,429	174,429	—	—
38	73	—	289,483	189,483	—	—
39	74	—	305,860	205,860	—	—
40	75	—	323,673	223,673	—	—

This proposal is for illustration purposes only. Figures quoted within are only projections and are not guarantees of future performance.

Maritime Life's Leveraged Premium Program

ASSUMPTIONS

Illustrations Rate:	8.00%
Before-Tax Loan Rate:	8.00%
Tax Rate:	50.00%
After-Tax Loan Rate:	4.00%
Maximum loan to CSV threshold:	75.00%

CLIENT DATA

Name	Age	Smoker	Sex	Product	Death age
John	50	N	M		
Mary	50	N	F		
Combined joint- age equivalent	37	N	M	Intrepid II	85

NET LOAN INTEREST

p = paid

c = capitalized

SINGLE PREMIUM DATA

Gross premium:	100,000
Premium duration:	1
SINGLE PREMIUM REQUIRED:	100,000

Policy duration	Beginning of Year Account value	Life CSV	Annual loan	Net loan interest	Taxable income	Tax payable	Cumulative loan	End of Year Annual outlay	Cumulative net outlay	Gross amount to estate	Net amount to estate	Net CSV
1	–	14,355	10,766	430c	–	–	11,197	89,233	89,233	702,000	690,802	4,306
2	–	29,574	10,983	887c	–	–	23,068	-10,983	78,249	758,160	735,091	8,872
3	–	45,784	11,269	1,373c	–	–	35,711	-11,269	66,979	818,813	783,101	13,735
4	–	64,617	12,751	1,938c	–	–	50,401	-12,751	54,228	884,317	833,915	19,385
5	–	86,437	14,426	2,593c	–	–	67,421	-14,426	39,801	955,063	887,641	25,931
6	–	111,827	16,449	3,354c	–	–	87,225	-16,449	23,352	1,031,468	944,242	33,548
7	–	122,074	4,329	3,662c	–	–	95,217	-4,329	19,022	974,783	879,565	36,622
8	–	132,251	3,971	3,967c	–	–	103,156	-3,971	15,051	939,398	836,241	39,675
9	–	143,407	4,399	4,302c	–	–	111,857	-4,399	10,652	918,070	806,212	43,022
10	–	153,780	3,477	4,613c	–	–	119,948	-3,477	7,174	898,295	778,346	46,134
11	–	165,337	4,053	4,960c	–	–	128,962	-4,053	3,120	888,477	759,514	49,601
12	–	178,192	3,120	5,283c	–	–	137,366	-3,120	–	886,691	749,324	55,081
13	–	192,474	–	5,494c	–	–	142,861	–	–	891,428	748,566	65,010
14	–	208,325	–	5,714c	–	–	148,575	–	–	901,985	753,409	76,416
15	–	225,902	–	5,943c	–	–	154,518	–	–	917,795	763,276	89,456
16	–	246,794	–	6,180c	–	–	160,699	–	–	942,830	782,130	105,838
17	–	270,000	–	6,427c	–	–	167,127	–	–	972,558	805,430	124,472
18	–	295,742	–	6,685c	–	–	173,812	–	–	1,006,763	832,950	145,589
19	–	324,272	–	6,952c	–	–	180,765	–	–	1,045,359	864,593	169,448
20	–	355,857	–	7,230c	–	–	187,995	–	–	1,088,508	900,512	196,330

Policy duration	Beginning of Year Account value	Life CSV	Annual loan	Net loan interest	Taxable income	Tax payable	Cumulative loan	End of Year Annual outlay	Cumulative net outlay	Gross amount to estate	Net amount to estate	Net CSV
21	—	390,786	—	7,519c	—	—	195,515	—	—	1,154,743	959,227	226,533
22	—	429,252	—	7,820c	—	—	203,336	—	—	1,225,006	1,021,669	260,256
23	—	471,565	—	8,133c	—	—	211,469	—	—	1,299,407	1,087,937	297,821
24	—	518,052	—	8,458c	—	—	219,928	—	—	1,377,922	1,157,993	339,568
25	—	569,071	—	8,797c	—	—	228,725	—	—	1,461,017	1,232,291	385,871
26	—	624,998	—	9,149c	—	—	237,874	—	—	1,548,905	1,311,030	437,123
27	—	686,227	—	9,514c	—	—	247,389	—	—	1,641,810	1,394,420	493,736
28	—	753,186	—	9,895c	—	—	257,285	—	—	1,739,974	1,482,688	556,155
29	—	826,329	—	10,291c	—	—	267,576	—	—	1,843,512	1,575,935	624,859
30	—	906,150	—	10,703c	—	—	278,279	—	—	1,952,867	1,674,587	700,363
31	—	992,585	—	11,131c	—	—	289,410	—	—	2,067,342	1,777,931	782,581
32	—	1,086,133	—	11,576c	—	—	300,987	—	—	2,187,202	1,886,214	872,036
33	—	1,187,337	—	12,039c	—	—	313,026	—	—	2,312,282	1,999,255	969,297
34	—	1,296,800	—	12,521c	—	—	325,547	—	—	2,443,320	2,117,772	1,074,997
35	—	1,415,183	—	13,021c	—	—	338,569	—	—	2,580,733	2,242,163	1,189,828
36	—	1,543,223	—	13,542c	—	—	352,112	—	—	2,724,942	2,372,829	1,314,568
37	—	1,681,746	—	14,084c	—	—	366,197	—	—	2,876,348	2,510,151	1,450,088
38	—	1,831,703	—	14,647c	—	—	380,844	—	—	3,034,814	2,653,969	1,597,395
39	—	1,994,219	—	15,233c	—	—	396,078	—	—	3,201,239	2,805,160	1,757,678
40	—	2,170,602	—	15,843c	—	—	411,921	—	—	3,376,266	2,964,344	1,932,329

| | Beginning of Year | | Annual loan | Net loan interest | Taxable income | Tax payable | Cumulative loan | End of Year | | | | |
Policy duration	Account value	Life CSV						Annual outlay	Cumulative net outlay	Gross amount to estate	Net amount to estate	Net CSV
41	—	2,362,414	—	16,476c	—	—	428,398	—	—	3,560,454	3,132,055	2,123,009
42	—	2,571,544	—	17,135c	—	—	445,534	—	—	3,754,378	3,308,843	2,331,733
43	—	2,800,315	—	17,821c	—	—	463,356	—	—	3,958,066	3,494,710	2,560,985
44	—	3,051,666	—	18,534c	—	—	481,890	—	—	4,172,649	3,690,758	2,813,909
45	—	3,329,295	—	19,275c	—	—	501,165	—	—	4,398,795	3,897,629	3,094,473
46	—	3,637,953	—	20,046c	—	—	521,212	—	—	4,637,119	4,115,906	3,407,777
47	—	3,983,849	—	20,848c	—	—	542,061	—	—	4,952,558	4,410,497	3,760,497
48	—	4,368,294	—	21,682c	—	—	563,743	—	—	5,367,758	4,804,014	4,154,014

• Worksheets only — Maritime Life will not be responsible for errors or omissions in the numbers provided.
• It is assumed that the single premium is placed in the Deposit Account.

Where bank loads are fully secured by life insurance, additional risk is inherent in the following assumptions:

• the difference (spread) between the assumed loan rate and the illustrated policy rate
• continued deductibility of interest on the loan
• life expectancy of the lives insured
• the rate credited to the policy

The maximum loan to cash value threshold is 95% of the portion of the cash value of the policy invested in interest-bearing accounts (Income Option, T-Bill Account, Portfolio Interest Option, or Fixed Interest Options). The threshold for the portion of the policy's cash value invested in index-linked options is 50%. This threshold may be higher in certain circumstances (e.g. Life Accumulator policy with the Stabilizer™ has a 75% threshold).

The Back-To-Back Guaranteed Investment Strategy

ASSUMPTIONS

a) $101,482.00 GIC/term deposit paying 5.0% annual has been included for comparison purposes only.

b) Marginal income tax rate of 46%

c) $100,000.00	Annuity with guaranteed lifetime income	
	Annual payout of:	$6,962.02
	Tax-exempt portion:	$4,499.55
d) $100,000.00	Term-to-100 level premium insurance coverage	
	Annual premium of:	$1,482.00
	Male	
	Non/Smoker	
	Age 65	

INVESTMENT PROPOSAL

TOTAL INVESTMENT TO BUY BACK-TO-BACK
$100,000.00

Annuity payment — received annually		$6,962.02
Insurance payment — paid annually	$1,482.00	
Income tax — paid annually	$1,132.74	
Amount of annuity payment remaining after tax & insurance		$4,347.28
Full TAX FREE return of original investment upon death		

If you were to buy a term deposit instead of this Back-to-Back
you would receive the following:

TOTAL INVESTMENT TO BUY TERM DEPOSIT
$100,000.00

Annual payment from term deposit		$5,074.10
Income tax — paid annually	$2,334.09	
Amount of payment remaining after tax		$2,740.01

Full return of original investment upon death
(less estate costs)

The Back-to-Back Investment Proposal contributes income of $1,607.27
per year more than a Term Deposit.

All death benefits from a Back-to-Back are TAX FREE
and paid directly to your beneficiary,
saving any costs to your estate.

GUARANTEED INVESTMENT STRATEGY

Prepared for male, 65, non-smoker

	GIC Comparison		Guaranteed Lifetime Annuity				
At age	GIC income after tax	GIC short fall	Annuity income after tax	Less premium amount	Net income after tax	Estate value after tax	Equivalent pre-tax return
67	2,740.01	(1,602.27)	5,829.28	1,482.00	4,347.28	100,000.00	7.93%
68	2,740.01	(1,602.27)	5,829.28	1,482.00	4,347.28	100,000.00	7.93%
69	2,740.01	(1,602.27)	5,829.28	1,482.00	4,347.28	100,000.00	7.93%
70	2,740.01	(1,602.27)	5,829.28	1,482.00	4,347.28	100,000.00	7.93%
71	2,740.01	(1,602.27)	5,829.28	1,482.00	4,347.28	100,000.00	7.93%
72	2,740.01	(1,602.27)	5,829.28	1,482.00	4,347.28	100,000.00	7.93%
73	2,740.01	(1,602.27)	5,829.28	1,482.00	4,347.28	100,000.00	7.93%
74	2,740.01	(1,602.27)	5,829.28	1,482.00	4,347.28	100,000.00	7.93%
75	2,740.01	(1,602.27)	5,829.28	1,482.00	4,347.28	100,000.00	7.93%
76	2,740.01	(1,602.27)	5,829.28	1,482.00	4,347.28	100,000.00	7.93%
77	2,740.01	(1,602.27)	5,829.28	1,482.00	4,347.28	100,000.00	7.93%
78	2,740.01	(1,602.27)	5,829.28	1,482.00	4,347.28	100,000.00	7.93%
79	2,740.01	(1,602.27)	5,829.28	1,482.00	4,347.28	100,000.00	7.93%
80	2,740.01	(1,602.27)	5,829.28	1,482.00	4,347.28	100,000.00	7.93%
81	2,740.01	(1,602.27)	5,829.28	1,482.00	4,347.28	100,000.00	7.93%
86	2,740.01	(1,602.27)	5,829.28	1,482.00	4,347.28	100,000.00	7.93%

	GIC Comparison		Guaranteed Lifetime Annuity				
At age	GIC income after tax	GIC short fall	Annuity income after tax	Less premium amount	Net income after tax	Estate value after tax	Equivalent pre-tax return
91	2,740.01	(1,602.27)	5,829.28	1,482.00	4,347.28	100,000.00	7.93%
96	2,740.01	(1,602.27)	5,829.28	1,482.00	4,347.28	100,000.00	7.93%
100	2,740.01	(1,602.27)	5,829.28	1,482.00	4,347.28	100,000.00	7.93%
105	2,740.01	($3,089.27)	$,829.28	—	5,829.28	100,000.00	10.64%
110	2,740.01	($3,089.27)	5,829.28	—	5,829.28	100,000.00	10.64%
115	2,740.01	($3,089.27)	5,829.28	—	5,829.28	100,000.00	10.64%
120	2,740.01	($3,089.27)	5,829.28	—	5,829.28	100,000.00	10.64%
125	2,740.01	($3,089.27)	5,829.28	—	5,829.28	100,000.00	10.64%